Business Strategy for a Better Normal

Photo by Armand Gilinsky

Armand Gilinsky

Business Strategy for a Better Normal

Concepts and Cases

palgrave
macmillan

Armand Gilinsky
Sonoma State University
Rohnert Park, CA, USA

ISBN 978-3-031-28707-7 ISBN 978-3-031-28708-4 (eBook)
https://doi.org/10.1007/978-3-031-28708-4

This Palgrave Macmillan imprint is published by the registered company Springer Nature Switzerland AG
The registered company address is: Gewerbestrasse 11, 6330 Cham, Switzerland

For Jo

Preface

The aim of this book is to provide students in capstone business courses and practitioners with an introduction to the most significant contemporary issues in strategic management. This book is based on my lectures in strategic management classes over 33 years and was developed via classroom testing of tools and supplementary exercises that prompted students to create their own strategic plans under conditions of increasing uncertainty. The material in this book is not intended to offer a compendium of all of myriad strategic issues faced by modern corporations and not-for-profit organizations.

Rohnert Park, USA | Armand Gilinsky

Acknowledgments

I am grateful to the support of Sonoma State University and F. Korbel & Bros. for partial funding to carry out the research for this book. Several colleagues provided valuable insights and revisions to chapter material for this book: Dr. Gina Grandy, Dr. Richard L. McCline, Dr. Sandra K. Newton, Dr. Renata Schafer, and Kaitlin Springmier. I also would like to thank the anonymous reviewers who offered many suggestions to make this book different and more current than previous strategy textbooks. Notably, Sarah Sperry Hehman provided valuable ideas, advice, and detailed editorial assistance from the beginning to the end of the project. Finally, I wish to thank my wife, Jo McCormick, and our sons, Allo and Michael, for their continuous support.

Praise for *Business Strategy for a Better Normal*

"This well-written textbook by an experienced strategist and expert case writer fills a gap in the current strategic management market. It does a great job of explaining all of the core strategic management concepts including external and industry analysis, strategic positioning (e.g., generic strategies), competitive advantage, diversification, and globalization. However, its real advantage is the care the author takes to introduce cutting edge concepts that are relevant right now in both management education and practice including the importance of diversity, equity and inclusion, the shifting norms related to work (coming out of the pandemic), and the fluid environment of global business resulting from changes in supply chain management. This textbook is both interesting and very readable. Students will enjoy it because chapters are to the point, include real-world examples and have cool cases at the end to apply the learning. Instructors will enjoy it because it is organized in a clear way and contains all of the key topics necessary for a robust course in strategic management!"

—Karin Schnarr, *Ph.D., Associate Professor, Strategic Management, Wilfrid Laurier University, Waterloo, Ontario, Canada*

"I highly recommend "Strategy for A Better Normal: Business Concepts & Cases" by Armand Gilinsky. This book provides a cutting-edge perspective on the present business terrain, offering a comprehensive guide for organizations to navigate the challenges and opportunities of today's rapidly changing world. With a unique focus on public interest and corporate social responsibility, readers will be empowered to develop innovative strategies that evolve with their industry and environment, ensuring sustainability and success. What sets this book apart is its innovative 3S Model of Style, Situation, and Strategic Orientation. This roadmap shows organizations how to craft strategies that can adapt to both their industry and the world around them, ensuring longevity and prosperity.

The book is well augmented with case studies and illustrative examples, illuminating how the key concepts can be brought to life in contemporary and relevant business contexts. For example, the case of DEI at Nike discusses the company's attempts to address criticism surrounding their diversity efforts and promote inclusivity, such as increasing representation of minorities and women and offering mental health support, as well as making DEI a responsibility for the entire workforce and a part of leadership's success metrics. Whether you are seeking to grow, improve, learn, or create a stronger value proposition for your customers, this book is a must-read for all professionals seeking to create a better "new normal" for their organizations. Armand Gilinsky's insightful and practical approach is a valuable resource for business leaders."

—William S. Silver, *President, Doobie Delivery, Boston, Massachusetts, USA*

"History will mark 2020 as a global socio-economic turning point that left many of us scratching our heads and wondering, "what *is* normal, anyway?" In "Strategy for a Better Normal," Dr. Gilinsky presents an array of contemporary business examples for which corporate strategy is evaluated through the lens of a changing post-pandemic landscape. His employment of strategic management tools offers strategists a variety of dynamic approaches to remaining competitive in today's ever-evolving global marketplace. Modern social and political themes such as sustainability, diversity and inclusion, physical and mental health, globalization, and technology are addressed as issues that can no longer be ignored by successful corporations.

As a winemaker entrenched in all aspects of wine production, marketing, and sales, Dr. Gilinsky's themes are particularly relevant to me. Never has the alcoholic beverage industry been so mission-based, with environmental, diversity and inclusion, technology, and innovation at the forefront of gatekeepers' and consumers' minds. The wine business is no longer solely about producing and selling delicious wines at a profit; offerings now need to offer societal and environmental benefits as well. The inclusion of multi-faceted values-driven strategies now underscores corporate profitability. Companies can no longer neglect the needs of their employees or the environment and stay relevant.

Dr. Gilinsky brings today's primary business and societal themes to life in a way that is both eloquent and engaging for the reader. Thought-provoking end-of-chapter exercises allow students to incorporate strategic concepts into practical, real-life activities. Business culture themes that may have been progressive a decade ago are harnessed into palatable, relatable cases that provide hope for "better normal" times ahead. Change and evolution have undeniably become the foundation of 21st-century business in the wine industry and beyond. "Strategy for a Better Normal" left me feeling challenged yet optimistic about navigating modern business challenges and further integrating values-driven strategies. I'll certainly raise a glass to that."

—Nicole Hitchcock, *Senior Winemaker at J Vineyards & Winery, Healdsburg, California, USA*

"Dr. Gilinsky's new strategy textbook portrays a refreshing take into traditional strategy frameworks, while expanding the spectrum of concepts and tools needed in the 21st century workplace such as DEI, de-globalization, supply chains, AI, the dark side of technology, and governance. End of the chapter mini-cases are not only current, but also relate to companies that students can easily recognize. These cases challenge the students to apply what they have learned in a real-world scenario, making the content of the book more relatable and applicable. Each chapter also includes an exercise/assignment to help students to reflect and build their own strategic plan. A valuable addition to every management professor's teaching portfolio!"

—Maria Ballesteros-Sola, *Ph.D., Associate Professor of Management, California State University Channel Islands, Camarillo, CA, USA*

"*Business Strategy for a Better Normal* is clear, succinct, and on point. Author Armand Gilinsky says the coronavirus pandemic required business leaders to make fast decisions (move employees home and online, rethink supply chain and inventory management, and serve customers in new ways, in order to generate new paths to profitability before the cash ran out). Emphasizing that innovation and continuous learning are more valuable capabilities than ever, each chapter shows students how traditional strategic management tools (Porter's Five Forces, Ansoff's Growth/Share Matrix, PESTLE, TOWS, other useful guiding frameworks) remain relevant. Gilinsky's "3 S" model provides a useful overall framework: Strategy aligns with an organization's current Situation (its political, economic, social, technological, legal and ecological context) and its Style (organizational culture, norms, propensities). Each chapter contains pertinent contemporary examples, a mini-case, and a personal-planning exercise that asks each student to reflect on their personal brand and helps them begin to plan a successful career that aligns with their personal style and situation. I especially appreciate that *Business Strategy for a Better Normal* is organized in nine chapters; it is only about 100 pages long. This gives adopting instructors latitude to assign some full-length strategy cases and relevant breaking-news articles for their MBA or undergraduate students to analyze and discuss."

—Janis Gogan, *Ph.D., Emeritus Professor of Information & Process Management, Bentley University, Waltham, MA, USA*

Contributors

I am grateful to the following people and organizations who provided learning content as well as written permission to include their cases and commentary in this book:

Chelsea Anderson, "Burbank Housing" (Chapter 2)

Grace Burroughs, "DEI at Nike, Inc." (Chapter 6)

Cinthya Cisneros (founder and CEO), Lisa Escalante, Caroline Evans, Julianna Flores, and Talia Gamble, "La Cheve Bakery and Brews" (Chapter 6)

Noe Espinoza and Alma Mendez, "La Texanita Mexican Restaurant" (Chapter 2)

Kayla Kremer, "Blue Apron" (Chapter 8)

Marielle MacDonell and Pat Hanson, (President), "Governance Challenges at North Bay Rowing Club" (Chapter 9)

Dr. Richard L. McCline (Chapter 6)

Michelle Parrish, "e.l.f. Beauty Faces Supply Chain Decisions" (Chapter 7)

Celine Zeyssolff, "Zeyssolff Winery" (Chapter 2)

Contents

About the Author

Armand Gilinsky Ph.D., recently completed 29 years of teaching strategic management, entrepreneurship, and wine business strategies at Sonoma State University in California. Prior to Sonoma State, he held teaching appointments at Northeastern University, the Harvard Business School, and California State University East Bay. He was appointed as the F. Korbel and Bros. Professor of Wine Business from 2014 to 2023. At Sonoma State, Dr. Gilinsky held appointments as Director of the Wine Business Institute, and Director of the Entrepreneurship Center. He received a university award from Excellence in Scholarship in 2013. Notable service activities have included a term as President of the North American Case Research Association in 2011, and as founding editor of the *Wine Business Journal* from 2014 to 2020. He has published over 50 case studies and 30 articles on strategy, social entrepreneurship, and wine businesses. He also worked with a study team to create a global marketing strategy for the Georgian wine industry, funded by the World Bank.

List of Figures

List of Tables

CHAPTER 1

Strategic Thinking

Abstract In this chapter, you will learn about mission, vision, goals, strategies, and tactics, and be introduced to the 3S Model consisting of Style, Situation, and Strategic Orientation.

Keywords Core values · Goals · Mission · Vision

Introduction

As the Cheshire Cat reminded Alice, in Lewis Carroll's *Alice in Wonderland* "If you don't know where you are going, any road will take you there." This book is about strategic thinking for organizations: setting goals and making choices. See Fig. 1.1, "A strategy-making hierarchy."

Vision and Mission

Organizational aspirations are typically debated, crafted, and codified by managers into a written mission or vision statement. An organization's vision statement refers to a desired possible "future state," while a mission statement is more commonly associated with the nature and scope of the business in the present, such as, why it exists and how it will

A. Gilinsky, *Business Strategy for a Better Normal*,
https://doi.org/10.1007/978-3-031-28708-4_1

Fig. 1.1 A strategy-making hierarchy (*Source* Created by author for this textbook)

manage risks to its survival (Ahlstrom et al., 2020; Hardy et al., 2020; Ketchen, 2020).

A **strategic vision** delineates management's aspirations for an organization, providing a panoramic view of "where we are going" and a convincing rationale for why this makes good business and societal sense. A strategic vision points an organization toward a particular direction, charts a strategic path for it to follow, builds commitment to the future course of action, and molds its identity. A clearly articulated strategic vision communicates management's aspirations to stakeholders (customers, employees, stockholders, suppliers, etc.) and helps steer the energies of an organization's talent in a common direction and build its culture. Chapter 2 takes up the issue of organizational culture in greater detail.

A **mission**, as defined by Peter Drucker (1974), is a declaration of an organization's reason for being and encapsulates its **core values**. Typically, a mission statement evolves from the intentions and beliefs of the founders that their organization can offer some product or service, to some customers, in some geographical area, using some type of technology, at a profitable price. As a business grows, a mission generally becomes formalized in writing and revised by subsequent managers in order to reflect the current state of affairs of the business (Pearce & David, 1987).

A mission has two major benefits. First, it is a rallying cry both inside and outside the firm. Often, employees complain that they never know what is happening. They don't know what the owner's plans are, nor how they, the employees, fit within those plans. This makes it difficult for them to be committed and motivated workers. A mission, often but not always in the form of a written statement, helps clarify the firm's vision and the employees' role in that vision. It's also important that owners/founders be able to clearly enunciate why the organization exists.

The second major benefit of a mission is the commitment made to preserving any organization's core values. It's like a New Year's resolution, but with higher stakes. If you make a resolution but tell no one, there is no particular incentive to keep it. But, if you discuss it, write it down, ponder it, type it up, post it on social media, tell your friends about it, maybe even wager that you will keep it, this public commitment means that you can't break it without losing face (or maybe money). In the same way, the written statement commits the company to the stated strategy and philosophy and may result in equal commitment by others in and around the business.

A **mission statement**, according to Campbell and Yeung (1991), helps establish an "emotional bond" between an organization and its stakeholders, thereby creating a collective core purpose, set of values, and buy-in on ways to achieve that core purpose, so that strategies that have been formulated may be implemented. By limiting its mission solely to deliver a product or service, an organization may miss the opportunity to create the emotional bond, sense of purpose, and resulting motivation that will be necessary to meet the intensified challenges in its industry.

A mission statement is dynamic. A mission must allow for flexibility and the ability to adapt to environmental changes while providing a unifying sense of purpose. As organizations are constantly evolving and external forces are changing, a mission statement needs to be periodically reviewed and revised (Greiner, 1972). Such a commitment in no way suggests that a company's mission is cast in stone, never to be altered. Missions, representing an organization's place in a dynamic environment and the strategies to achieve success, often change over time. Change happens as an organization assesses movements in its macro-environment and competitive situation, as will be discussed in Chapter 3, and reconsiders what's absolutely critical to achieve. Inertia and inability to change can lead to underperformance and failure.

A mission thus provides the core values, central focus, and unifying drive for an organization's strategic management system—comprised of goals, strategies, and tactics—altogether intended for a long-term planning horizon under conditions of great uncertainty (Foss, 2020). See Table 1.1 for examples of company missions and visions. Absent that system, an organization is unlikely to accomplish much and may be unsustainable.

Goals, Strategies, and Tactics

Goals are "what" organizations seek to attain or become. Goals may include growth, stability, and pulling back (also known as retrenchment). Some goals (also known as objectives) can be measured, such as sales revenue growth, profits and margins, market share, employee and customer retention, stock price appreciation, capital accumulation, donations, and so forth. Other goals can be more difficult to measure, such as brand equity, customer satisfaction, employee morale, leadership effectiveness, etc.

Strategy is the "how" or potential choices of direction toward attaining a goal or set of goals. It is a "best guess" or hypothesis about the future effectiveness of any steps taken toward goals. How might these steps be worded? Table 1.2 shows several examples of strategies that address an organization's short- and long-term time horizons, also known as their current customer-markets and future customer-markets.

Tactics. These are the specific action items requiring deployment of resources and capabilities (see Chapter 4) that can enable organizations to stay on course toward achieving a strategy (deWitte, 2021).

A Better Proposition

Since early 2020, life activities appear to have taken on a strange new rhythm in a seemingly rhythmless world. We've been living in abnormal times and are all wondering what it means and how it will play out.

Table 1.1 Examples of company missions and visions

Company	*Mission*	*Vision*
AirBnB	"To create a world where anyone can belong anywhere and we are focused on creating an end-to-end travel platform that will handle every part of your trip"	"Belong anywhere"
Athleta	"To ignite a community of active, healthy, confident women and girls who empower each other to reach their limitless potential"	"We're here to empower women and girls."
Chick-fil-A	"To be America's best quick-service restaurant at winning and keeping customers"	"To glorify God by being a faithful steward of all that is entrusted to us. To have a positive influence on all who come in contact with Chick-fil-A"
Friedman's Home Improvement	"We are Born to Connect, Lead, Grow, Serve & Care"	"We strive to deliver the human side of home improvement"
GameStop	"Together, we hold a passion for gaming, a commitment to our industry and a disciplined business perspective to continuously drive value with shareholders, customers, vendors, and employees"	
LinkedIn	"Connect the world's professionals to make them more productive and successful"	"Create economic opportunity for every professional in the world through the developing initiative of the Economic Graph, a digital representation of the global economy"
Lululemon	"Elevate the world from mediocrity to greatness"	"Be the experimental brand that ignites a community of people living the sweat life through sweat, grow and connect"

(continued)

Table 1.1 (continued)

Company	*Mission*	*Vision*
Sephora	**"We believe beauty is for each person to define and ours to celebrate. Together, we support and encourage bold choices in beauty—and in life. Our purpose is to inspire fearlessness"**	"Be the change-maker in the beauty sector and create a worthwhile experience for all customers"
Tesla	"To accelerate the advent of sustainable transport by bringing compelling mass-market electric cars to market as soon as possible"	"To create the most compelling car company of the 21st century by driving the world's transition to electric vehicles"
Ulta Beauty	We're on a quest to bring the fun side of beauty to all—constantly delighting our guests with All Things Beauty, All in One Place™ while offering rewarding careers for our passionate, beauty-loving associates. Every day we use the power of beauty to bring to life the possibilities that lie within each of us—inspiring every guest and enabling each associate to build a fulfilling career	To be the most-loved beauty destination of our guests and the most-admired retailer by our Ulta Beauty associates, communities, partners and investors

Sources Company websites

> There are three reasons why the new normal might be better than the old normal. Last week I heard a CEO say that his team had a task force working the past three years to create a digital strategy; once this crisis took hold, they had it launched in just 10 days. We don't want to be reckless, but we can't go back to business as usual. We have to keep the urgency that makes things happen. It will be critical to surviving the next year. There is something about a crisis that pushes us back to our mission. We all want to help take care of each other and our customers. We feel a tremendous responsibility to do something. (Litton, 2020)

It feels right to take a pause to re-evaluate and reset our life purpose: missions, visions, goals, and directions toward those goals. Striving to achieve a "better normal" in our lives after 2020 will require more than

Table 1.2 Examples of competitive strategies

Current customer-markets	*Future customer-markets*
Concentrate on serving a *well-defined customer group* and offer a portfolio of products specially tailored to meet their needs	Recruit and retain high-caliber talent by *offering pay and conditions well above the industry average*
Serve a *local market or markets* where we have a convenient location, better knowledge of the area, or lower freight costs than national suppliers	*Create a new product concept*, thus creating a new market segment
Invest in new technology to improve our products and services and also make our business more efficient	Develop the capability to act more quickly, to be *more flexible and more responsive to customer needs* than rivals
Remain a *smaller, more flexible organization* with lower overheads and tighter controls than our competitors	Enter into *joint ventures with other organizations* to get access to new capital, customers, and/or technology
Obtain *exclusive rights* to a product (or market) because of specialized know-how, copyrights, exclusive design, patents, a license, or a franchise	*Acquire* other companies to boost market share and/or obtain access to new markets
Provide a valuable product or service to a large manufacturer or distributor on a *sub-contract* basis	Sell a range of products to the same types of customers in *new markets overseas*
Use *tight financial controls* to meet operating benchmarks	Identify opportunities in growth markets and *enter these markets early*

Source Taylor et al. (1990)

resiliency in the face of crises just past and yet to come, in order to maintain continuity and sustainability. It will require a plan (Scranton, 2021). In the words of Jennifer Ashton (as quoted by Anahad O'Connor in *The New York Times*), "Nothing that we are doing today or have lived through in the last year [2020] is normal" (O'Connor, 2021).

This book will expose you to strategic planning, public interest (responsible business models), corporate social responsibility, managing in times of crisis, demographics (act locally), company culture, and provide you with the analytical tools to help you navigate among the many choices that organizations, both for-profit and not-for-profit, need to make to sustain themselves.

An organization's value proposition represents a promise of value to be delivered, communicated, and acknowledged. That proposition also represents a belief from the organization's customers and other actors involved with the organization, known as stakeholders, about how value will be delivered, experienced, and acquired.

As one observer of the wine industry put it, in order to meet the expectations and needs of stakeholders, organizations need to learn from recent adversity and create better, stronger value propositions.

> Worrying is like a rocking chair—it gives you something to do but it doesn't get you anywhere. I don't want things to go back to normal and you shouldn't either. "Normal" was not good for our industry [wine] and despite the challenges that lay ahead, ultimately, I'm of the opinion that most will come out the other side of this crisis stronger and more confident than they were going in. If you look for doom and gloom, you will find it; but if you seek out the opportunities to grow, improve, learn and provide a stronger value proposition for your customers, you will find more of them than you can poke a stick at. (Owens, 2020: 79)

How will organizations be able to grow, improve, learn, and provide a stronger, better value proposition? According to Sebastian Seung, president and head of Samsung Research, "We are at the beginning of a very unique opportunity to not just overcome the past year's adversity, but to create a Better Normal for All, and I'm so excited to share more about how Samsung is making this a reality" (Samsung Press Release, 2021).

The remainder of this book and the cases accompanying the chapters are organized around a novel triumvirate of strategic thinking concepts for the better normal, a **3S Model: Style, Situation, and Strategic Orientation**. The environment (*situation*) creates or deters opportunities that are pursued by strategists with the propensity (*style*) and the potential (*strategy*) to develop them. In order to be sustainable and successful, an organization's strategy needs to evolve along with the style of its top management team and the situation or perceived environment affecting all rivals in its industry or sphere of operations.

The following chapters describe how to plan under urgent as well as more placid conditions, scan the external environment, build community, pursue innovation, and build a consensus among diverse groups on implementing the plan (Thomas and Parris, 2021).

End of Chapter Example: Missions and Visions of Leading Consumer Companies

Mission statements of leading consumer brands can be found at: https://ebaqdesign.medium.com/mission-statements-of-top-brands-9343e697db74.

Lessons learned. With society's growing focus on diversity, equity, and inclusion (DEI), many companies are asking what role they can play. Compared to the statements above, Johnson & Johnson's mission statement is a good example of a company philosophy and policy commitment to DEI [see: https://www.jnj.com/about-jnj/policies-and-positions/diversity-equity-and-inclusion-policy].

Research suggests that mission and vision statements tend to indicate the presence of policies and procedures that could correlate to stronger diversity metrics. Here are two examples.

An August 2021 Morgan Stanley Institute for Sustainable Investing survey found that 71% of individual investors identified multicultural diversity, incorporating elements of race, ethnicity, and culture, as an area of interest for their portfolios. Beyond the benefits to society, diversity matters because achieving balance in representation, empowerment, and economic opportunity can also boost financial outcomes.

According to a 2020 study from McKinsey & Co., companies with the most gender-diverse teams were 25% more likely to have above-average profitability, and companies with the most ethnically diverse teams were 36% more likely to outperform as measured by earnings before interest and taxes.

End of Chapter Strategic Planning Exercise

My Strategy Plan

As you work through this book, there will be opportunities for you to build your own strategic plan. Create a 90-second video "selfie" using your mobile phone, or tablet, or computer. In your video, please answer the following three (3) questions:

1. What are your expectations for this course, that is, what are your goals?

2. Describe an accomplishment of which you are most proud. How has this helped you find a mission in life?
3. If you had one year to live, assuming no financial hardship and good health during that year, what would you do and why? Craft a strategic vision statement for yourself.

Further Reading

Ahlstrom, D., Arreghle, J.-L., Hitt, M., Qian, G., Ma, Z., & Faems, D. (2020). Managing technological, sociopolitical, and institutional change in the new normal. *Journal of Management Studies, 57*(3), 411–437.

Campbell, A., & Yeung, S. (1991). Creating a sense of mission. *Long Range Planning, 24*(4), 10–20.

deWitte, M. (2021, March 22). *Hitting the reset button: Stanford psychologist says we can build a better normal after the pandemic*. Stanford News online. Retrieved May 5, 2021 from: https://news.stanford.edu/2021/03/22/hitting-reset-button-building-better-normal-pandemic/

Drucker, P. (1974). *Management: Tasks, responsibilities, and practices*. Harper & Row.

Foss, N. J. (2020). Behavioral strategy and the COVID-19 disruption. *Journal of Management, 46*(8), 1322–1329.

Greiner, L. (1972, July–August). Evolution and revolution as organizations grow. *Harvard Business Review*, 37–46.

Hardy, C., Maguire, S., Power, M., & Tsoukas, H. (2020). Organizing risk: Organization and management theory for the risk society. *Academy of Management Annals, 14*(2), 1032–1066. https://doi.org/10.5465/annals.2018.0110

Ketchen, D. J., Jr. (2020). Research at the intersection of entrepreneurship, supply chain management, and strategic management: Opportunities highlighted by COVID-19. *Journal of Management, 46*(8), 1330–1341.

Litton, S. (2020, April 24). *The coronavirus is changing what 'normal' means for businesses around the world. Here are 3 ways it could become a change for the better*. Entrepreneur. Retrieved May 5, 2021 from: https://www.businessinsider.com/3-reasons-why-new-normal-may-be-change-for-better-2020-4

O'Connor, A. (2021, April 16). Gearing up for the 'new normal.' *The New York Times*. Retrieved May 5, 2021 from: https://www.nytimes.com/2021/04/16/well/mind/jennifer-ashton-new-normal-building-resilience.html

Owens, W. (2020, May). The best is yet to come: Practical online strategies to grow wine sales in the 'new normal.' *Australian and New Zealand Grapegrower and Winemaker, 876*, 78–79.

Pearce, J., II., & David, F. (1987). Corporate mission statements: The bottom line. *Academy of Management Executive, 1*(2), 109–116.

Samsung Corp Press Release. (2021, January 11). *Samsung introduces latest innovations for a better normal at CES 2021.* Retrieved May 5, 2021 from: https://news.samsung.com/us/ces-2021-better-normal/

Scranton, R. (2021, January 25). I've said goodbye to 'normal.' You should, too. *The New York Times*. Retrieved January 25, 2021 from: https://www.nytimes.com/2021/01/25/opinion/new-normal-climate-catastrophes.html

Taylor, B., Gilinsky, A., Hilmi, A., Hahn, D., & Grab, U. (1990). Strategy and leadership in growth companies. *Long Range Planning, 23*(3), 66–75.

Thomas, E., & Parris, A. (2021, August 2). DEI signal: Assessing managers on diversity, equity and inclusion. In *On the markets* (Morgan Stanley Investors Report, pp. 10–11).

CHAPTER 2

Organizational Cultures

Abstract In this chapter, you will learn about organizational cultures, leadership styles, and why it is vital for strategic managers to be proactive in order to focus on future customer and market needs.

Keywords Culture · Distinctive competencies · Proactive vs. reactive · Style · Turnaround

Developing a Strategy

Developing a strategy for an organization is beset by tensions between external market pressures to continue rapid growth (also known as macro-environmental and competitive forces, which will be covered in Chapter 3) and the internal pressures to maintain tradition or pursue innovation (which will be covered in Chapter 4).

Many organizations walk a tightrope, balancing the preservation of an established high-quality brand image, hometown culture, and equity with any future opportunities to become more multi-cultural, more innovative, and more inclusive.

Corporate culture is the number one recruiting tool used by companies today.

A. Gilinsky, *Business Strategy for a Better Normal*,
https://doi.org/10.1007/978-3-031-28708-4_2

One company Founder and CEO, Jim Rosen of Fantastic Foods, told the author that:

> Culture is like yogurt: once you start growing it, it is unstoppable. We give our staff tough but not insurmountable tasks to build self-esteem and good attitudes, get them up to speed then let them do the job entirely themselves, let employees follow through on ideas and suggestions whenever possible, even if you have doubts, look for opportunities for staff to learn on their own, set benchmarks, such as daily productions goals which act as automatic feedback. I personally—and the whole company, because I've given it some of its personality—focus on doing an excellent job at everything we do.

All organizations are striving to develop distinctive competencies (valued, rare, and otherwise) to overtake established rivals.

The relationships among environments, company managers, organizational cultures, and strategic decision-making are complex and often difficult to tease out. As we will discover in Chapter 3, the environment (*situation*) creates or deters opportunities that are pursued by managers with the propensity (*style*) and the potential (*strategy*) to develop them. Achieving consensus on and harmony among these attributes may positively (or negatively) impact an organization's growth.

Organizational cultures are often impacted by the guiding tendencies and values of their leaders, whose styles can be depicted as a continuum anchored by "Managerial" on one end, and "Entrepreneurial" on the other. See Fig. 2.1.

Quadrants

A. Organizations who are guided by technocrats, guided by meeting objectives, and seek placid or stable environments, such as Fortune 500 corporations.

   Example: United Parcel Service (UPS). Carol Tomé, incoming CEO of UPS in 2020, who told a CNBC reporter in June 2021, "The stock price had been flat for about six years. I'm like, I think I could get in there and swizzle the business model a little bit and create some value. We are an engineering-driven company, we are so method-driven, so process-driven, that's why we're the best in the world at what we do," Tomé said. "We weren't actually

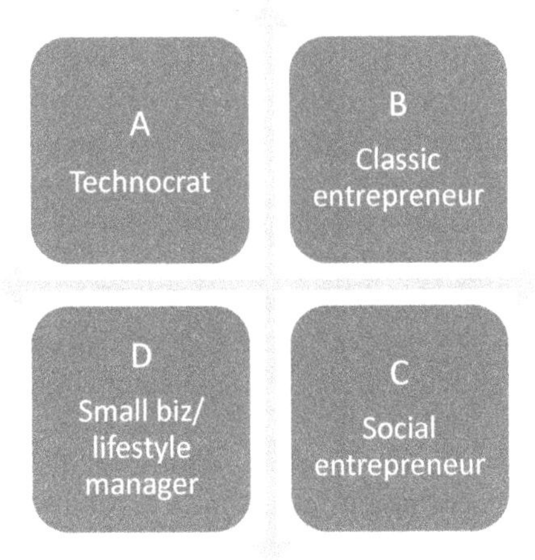

Fig. 2.1 Mapping strategic leadership styles (*Source* Created by author)

empowering our people for innovation. In fact, we were very much command and control, we're telling people what to do, rather than listening," she added (Thomas, 2021).

B. Organizations are led by classic entrepreneurs that pursue high-growth opportunities via innovations and assemble the resources and capabilities to bring them to market, such as technology startups.

   Example: Stitch Fix. In 2011, Katrina Lake founded Stitch Fix, a leading online personal styling service, when she was a Harvard Business School student. Lake took the company public in 2017, and in doing so was the youngest woman at the time to ever take a company public. Since then, Lake has grown Stitch Fix into an industry leading business with an annual revenue of $1.7bn, serving nearly four million clients across the U.S. and U.K., employing 8,000 people, and shipping thousands of personalized items of apparel every day. In April 2021, Lake was succeeded as CEO and appointed Executive Chairperson of the Board. Lake recalled, "In founding Stitch Fix, I was inspired by a very human problem, to help people look and feel their best by finding clothes they love. Ten years into this journey, I'm even more inspired by this simple mission, proud of the way we've delivered against it, and incredibly optimistic about our future" (Stitch Fix company press release, April 13, 2021).

C. Organizations are led by intrepid entrepreneurs seeking change but building ventures without a safety net of capital or endowments, such as social ventures and beneficial corporations, also known as "B Corps."

Example: Burbank Housing. Burbank Housing is a non-profit affordable housing company in the North Bay region, about 50 miles from San Francisco, California. Burbank Housing's mission statement read: "we are a local nonprofit dedicated to building quality affordable housing in the North Bay. We create vibrant local communities that are carefully designed, professionally managed, and sustainable both financially and environmentally, to foster opportunities for people with limited-income of all ages, backgrounds, and special needs." The organization also believed in four core values: community, integrity, compassion, and teamwork. As stated in its strategic plan, community for Burbank Housing meant they "actively engaged with people and institutions to share information, ideas, and resources in order to help others achieve their goals." Yet Burbank Housing's goals of increasing cash flows was becoming more even more difficult to achieve, despite the uptick in demand for affordable housing after major regional fires in 2017, 2019, and 2020. Though the organization subsisted on collecting cash from development fees and property management (rentals) and putting the money aside for development projects, its existential challenge was determining and optimizing the internally generated cash flows needed for development without having to resort to external financing via grants and endowments. Internally, Burbank Housing's staff desired more training on information systems and team building activities to motivate and promote more effective teamwork. An increase of two-way internal communication was also requested by many employees throughout the organization. Property managers had been particularly vocal about their desire for communication concerning what was going on at the main office. Monthly newsletters had been the norm in the past, but those had been discontinued. Company-wide informational meetings had not been held since 2017 (Anderson & Gilinsky, 2022).

D. Organizations are led by technicians who are "in the business," such as small or family or lifestyle businesses.

Example: La Texanita Mexican Restaurant. In June 2020, Alma Mendez, the owner of La Texanita in Sonoma County, California, was overwhelmed because she was finding it difficult to make ends meet. Because her restaurant sales had declined 43% in the first three months of the COVID-19 pandemic, she was barely making enough money to stay open and did not know if things were going to get worse or better. Mendez's goal had always been to open up a second location. Mendez related: "When Guy Fieri came over in June of 2009 and did an episode of *Diners, Dives, and Drive-ins*, it opened the door for me. Before, local Hispanics were my only customers. After the episode aired on the Food Network, tourists and a more diverse group of patrons started to come and dine in. Consequently, my restaurant got a lot busier than what it already was, and lots of people would be waiting outside in a line to come in to have a bite, others would simply leave because they did not want to wait, and there was nothing I could do about it. Fast-forward 10 years later to August of 2019: Guy Fieri called me again and said he wanted to do a follow-up episode on how La Texanita had evolved over the years, and he also said the episode would not air until spring of 2020. Right then and there I knew it was the right time to open up our second location in 2020 because it was going to have the same effect as it did 10 years ago, lots of new customers, and this time I was going to capitalize on the opportunity. It's been almost three months since the shelter-in-place was ordered, we hope that we can sustain the restaurant with current sales, but will that be enough to be able to open a second location?" Mendez wondered (Espinoza, 2020).

Style and Strategy

Entrepreneurial. This style is driven by the presence or generation of opportunities for new entry into industries and markets, but tends to be less concerned about the resources that may be required to pursue such opportunities. Entrepreneurial strategy begins before a company is even formed. It (should) starts at the "idea" phase of the life cycle of the business (Covin and Slevin, 1990). Assembling and marshaling the necessary resources represent a secondary step for the entrepreneurially managed firm and perhaps part of the thinking about the implementation of discovered opportunities (Stevenson et al., 1989). The presence or lack of resources does not constrain the strategic thinking of an entrepreneurially managed firm.

The leadership styles of many entrepreneurs not only tend to be more or less similar (hands-on control and self-determination), but also can differ based on the personality characteristics and circumstances of each entrepreneur. In general, entrepreneurs tend to be task-oriented, drive themselves and others relentlessly, and yet have charismatic personalities that inspire others. They tend to have high achievement motives, high enthusiasm and creativity, and don't care for bureaucracy. They see opportunities before others and want to act quickly when the opportunities arise. Still, entrepreneurs tend to be impatient with other people and do not suffer fools gladly.

Managerial. These administrative-type leaders, by contrast, need rules and hierarchies. They are more apt to follow the lead of other firms, imitate best practices, manage by objectives, and possess qualities not often found in entrepreneurs (Miles and Snow, 1978; Miles et al., 1993). One might say that the entrepreneurs are the idea people, and the managers keep the organization working.

Table 2.1 illustrates the defining traits of these **strategic leadership styles**.

Before diving into how to use strategic management tools for analysis, we probably should take some time to recap key features of an organization's culture and how those features might impact—positively or negatively—any planned continuance or change in the future.

These features include:

- Values, business principles, and ethical standards;
- Official policies, procedures, and practices guiding employee behavior;
- Atmosphere and spirit;
- How managers and employees interact;
- Strength of peer pressure;
- Actions and behaviors that are explicitly encouraged and rewarded;
- Revered traditions and "heroic acts";
- How the company deals with external stakeholders; and

Table 2.1 Typologies of strategic leadership styles

Leadership style	*Defining traits*	*Characteristics*
Entrepreneurial	"Pioneers"	Strategic decisions consist of emergent "trial and error" approaches and adjustments. Strategies are based on creativity and intuition (right brain), attempting to gauge the direction of change "without investing heavily in information." This "intrepid" style of leadership is considered to be high-risk
Entrepreneurial	"Value innovators"	Strategic decisions are considered to be agents for change and innovation. The strategist formulates intended strategies focused on "intended high performance goals" as the final effects of change become more apparent. Business leaders plan how to manage risks to obtain rewards
Managerial	"Avoiders"	Given a perceived placid or benign environment, the leader bases strategic decisions on an "if it ain't broke, don't fix it," mentality, driven by security, stability, and risk reduction
Managerial	"Technocrats"	Strategic decisions are part of an overall corporate or business structure. Strategy is planned. No moves are made "unless an internal consensus is reached" or "an entire information set coming from the industry is taken into consideration before a decision is reached." This is similar to the "rational expectations" literature in economics; using all information for each decision defines the leader as low-risk and rational (left brain)

Source Adapted by author from Naman and Slevin (1993)

- Strength and genuineness of the commitment to corporate citizenship and environmental sustainability.

Celine Zeyssolff, a co-owner of Zeyssolff Winery, a family-owned and family-run business in Alsace, France, commented on her company's culture in a Zoom conversation in June 2020, during the early months of the COVID-19 pandemic:

> There are some companies that give up, a lot will lay their employees off and for me the important decision will be to be able… to take the risk to

maintain all my activity when we currently have no business (laughs) and that's a decision that's quite difficult to make, to think 'well, let's carry on as if we had a hundred customers a day when we only have maybe 10 at best,' and... but I think that it's worth it. I mean, I remain convinced that this situation is transitory and that we need to hang in there. I've always hung in there and I think COVID won't stop me (laughs). So, this is an important decision, at least for a small company like us, to keep a wage bill that's greater than our current needs.

Types of Organizational Cultures

Strongly implanted cultures. These assist in executing strategy because company managers can use the traditions, beliefs, values, common bonds, or behavioral norms as levers to mobilize commitment to executing the chosen strategy. Companies that are able to develop a strong culture have: (1) a founder or strong leader who establishes core values, principles, and practices that are viewed as having contributed to the success of the company, and (2) a sincere, long-standing company commitment to operating the business according to these established traditions and values.

Weak corporate cultures. These provide little or no assistance in executing strategy because there are no traditions, beliefs, values, common bonds, or behavioral norms that management can use as levers to mobilize commitment to executing the chosen strategy.

A company culture that is consistent with the requirements for good strategy execution can energize employees, deepen their commitment to execute the strategy flawlessly, and enhance worker productivity in the process. But an unhealthy culture can be:

Change-resistant. These avoid risk, place a premium on not making mistakes, maintain the status quo, protect the power base, and guard their immediate interests;

Politicized. These are characterized by empire-building managers that pursue their own agendas, protect their own turf, and operate work units as autonomous "fiefdoms";

Insular/inwardly focused. These cultures discount the merits of what outsiders are doing and to see little payoff from studying best-in-class performers;

Unethical/greed focused. These typically have an "ends-justifies-the-means" mentality, and are prone to adopt accounting principles that make financial performance look better than it really is; and **Characterized by clashing subcultures.** These are plagued by internal jockeying for power, lacking consensus, exhibiting fragmented or inconsistent approaches to strategy implementation.

Leaders in culture-building or crisis situations demonstrate several characteristics that may dictate whether or not a leader can succeed in the effort. The length of CEO tenure is negatively related to rebounds in performance: declining firms with longer tenured CEOs will have a significant challenge in terms of orchestrating the appropriate (and sometimes drastic) strategic response needed in crisis situations. According to Abebe (2009), firms with CEOs who have output-related functional backgrounds (e.g., marketing, sales, and R&D) exhibit better turnaround performance compared to those firms led by CEOs that have significant throughput-related functional backgrounds (e.g., operations, production, engineering, and accounting).

Finally, leaders of troubled firms can increase the likelihood of engaging all organizational members to help when a crisis looms by: (a) Solidifying personal leverage (via securing board support, managing expectations, under-promising, and over-delivering), (b) setting the stage for change (via articulation of objectives and expectations, explaining the plight, and illustrating an existential challenge); (c) generating open dialogue (via practicing participatory leadership, acknowledging reflective responses, and walking the talk); (d) stabilizing the situation (via halting the hemorrhage, optimizing talent, and removing bureaucratic clutter); and (e) spawning success (via facilitating opportunities for learning, monitoring the organization's momentum, and reinforcing and rewarding people to incentivize results) (Boyd, 2011). Nearly every portrayal of successful leaders that attempted a cultural turnaround raised the question of cultural consonance: "Am I happy with the job?" Now, that's the killer question!

Why Strategists Need to Be Forward-Looking

It is commonly accepted that at the organizational level, the articulation of a mission, objectives, and strategies is the starting point for change.

Without a unifying guiding vision, every employee—managers included—will provide their own rationale for every decision they make. Without a unifying guiding concept or mission, it is unlikely that these rationales will coincide, and it is equally unlikely that the collective decisions will produce consistent results or move the organization in a consistent direction. For these reasons, the available research indicates that organizations characterized by well-defined, well-communicated missions that emanate from organizational culture and values and that drive organizational design, generally outperform those firms that have not developed these tools. Some organizations have recently learned the hard way that their systems are endangered because of a reactive, almost lackadaisical approach to strategy.

On the other hand, being proactive (or forward-looking) means more than simply thinking about the future of an organization. Strategists must also contend with taking actions to focus on future customer-market needs, including needs which customers may not yet have identified for themselves. Who knew that we would be making such a rapid transition in 2020 to the Zoom economy and that corporate staff would begin to move away from the cities to smaller "Zoom towns"? (Smith, 2020). Strategic foresight is the ability to anticipate discontinuities in [the] business environment as well as the threats and opportunities in the enterprise and any impending disruptive moves to be made by competitors.

Consensus on mission and vision, strategy, and key success factors is forged based on the beliefs and values and needs of an organization's multiple stakeholders. Sometimes, however, consensus among stakeholders can be elusive, particularly in organizations with unhealthy or weak cultures.

As you diagnose and prescribe strategies for organizations in this course, please consider how the disparate needs and expectations of all stakeholders may sometimes come into conflict—or be brought to a consensus.

Also consider where to compete, not just how to compete. The "where," of course, depends on factors in an organization's macro- and competitive environments. Chapter 3 begins coverage of these factors with a presentation of some important environmental scanning tools used in strategic management.

End of Chapter Mini-Case: How Airbnb Built Its Belonging Culture

Armand Gilinsky

Persons walking into the Airbnb headquarters in its South of Market Street (SOMA) location in San Francisco might believe that they were entering a trendy inner-city apartment building in almost any place in the world. This setting is deliberately aligned with the company's vision: "(to create a world where you can) Belong anywhere."

Looking out across the atrium-like foyer from inside HQ, visitors peer into a kaleidoscope of colorful rooms that were painstakingly built to resemble some of the more interesting Airbnb homes from around the world, including the founder's apartment where the company started, all marked proudly with a plaque telling the story of the actual host and home.

Airbnb's former Head of Employee Experience, Mark Levy, explained at a lecture for Culture Amp clients that his company had an epiphany of sorts in July 2020: "We've focused on starting with our employees, and shifted them up the commitment curve, to the point now where we talk about how we treat our employees like founders," Levy said in an April 2020 YouTube video presentation to the HR Congress.

Creating an Open Dialogue at Work

The culture Airbnb managed to create was underpinned by not only its commitment to its mission and values but also to its unrelenting belief in honest, two-way communication. "Our rule of thumb is that nobody should hear about anything externally until we've told them internally," Levy insisted.

Airbnb employees (they call them "Airfam") joined a bi-weekly world meeting, which was typically out of San Francisco. People from outside of the San Francisco office join that meeting through a live stream. Each country or city office also held a more informal meeting toward the end of the week. As for the executive team, they meet weekly. Levy's job is to get notes from the executive meeting to every person in the company

A. Gilinsky
Sonoma State University, Rohnert Park, CA, USA

within 24 hours of that meeting. "We distribute [the notes] very broadly and people really appreciate knowing what we're talking about and ask questions, share thoughts and ideas," Levy said. "That stems from our communication philosophy that we want to have an honest, open, and two-way dialogue between everyone in the company," Levy added.

Bringing Company Culture to Life

Airbnb subsequently developed and launched an intranet to update everyone on employee birthdays and anniversaries. It also hosted a web page for each employee and office so people got to know one other and build their internal networks.

Levy noted that the company's other "secret sauce" was a group called "ground control" that formed a part of the employee experience team. The team's aim was to bring Airbnb's culture to life. Members were tasked with looking after the workplace environment, internal communications, employee recognition, celebrations, and workplace events. The team was comprised up of over 10 people in San Francisco, and the role existed in just about every one of the Airbnb offices around the world.

"It's one of those things in that they are not 'forcing fun', we are reinforcing and supporting how we bring the culture alive," Levy noted. "We do it through pop-up birthday celebrations, anniversaries, or baby showers as well as creatively themed events based on holidays or events." For example, the company celebrated Pride month as well as Airbnb's entry into the market in Cuba. "It's simply thoughtful and caring people paying attention to it in a way that's culturally relevant - bringing our global travel mindset and mission to life," Levy noted. "We remember that we need to have a full life and we integrate work with what's going on in the world."

Recruiting and Onboarding at Airbnb

It was not unusual for Airbnb to receive over 180,000 resumes for only 900 position openings. "We're both lucky and quite challenged," Levy was quoted as saying (Bovim, 2019).

Every candidate that made it through to the interview process underwent a set of interviews related to their prospective role. Candidates also had to undergo two additional interviews related to core values. These conversations were conducted by people who were outside of the function for which they were interviewing, who were selected for interviewing by the company's founders, and who talked with the candidates about their experience, understanding, and mindset related to Airbnb.

Levy noted that Airbnb was looking for "missionaries, not mercenaries." He offered this advice for would-be applicants: "The minute people start talking about job titles or are more interested in the equity over changing the world through connecting people via local and authentic travel experiences, we know that they are probably barking up the wrong tree. We're very true to our core values in the hiring process" (Bovim, 2019).

Once somebody made it through both sets of interviews and received an offer, they went through a week-long check-in process that focused on the Airbnb values, business strategies, an introduction to each function, and ways of working. New team members usually went through this process with others who have also been recently hired. "We create belonging by enabling them to form a group that hopefully stays together as they progress here through their careers," Levy said in the lecture for Culture Amp. He continued, "We schedule different kinds of lunches and meetings to help people to understand the colleagues they're going to be working with. We ask all new hires to share a fun fact and why they came to work here, not just about their job, but who they are, what they are into, and how they ended up working at Airbnb."

Lessons learned. Culture is a company's internal work climate or organizational DNA, and it is shaped by its core values, beliefs, chemistry, ingrained behaviors, "how we do things around here," and business principles. Every company, Airbnb included, has its own unique corporate culture—the shared values, ingrained attitudes, and company traditions that determine norms of behavior, accepted work practices, and styles of operating. The character of a company's culture is a product of the core values and beliefs that executives espouse, "the tone that is set at the top," the standards of what is ethically acceptable and what is not, the chemistry and the personality that permeate the work environment, the company's traditions, and the stories that get told over and over to illustrate and reinforce the company's shared values, business practices, and traditions. In a very real sense, Airbnb's culture is the company's automatic, self-replicating operating system that defines "how we do things around here." Many company founders and executives want the work climate at their companies to mirror certain values and ethical standards, partly because of their own personal convictions, but mainly because they are convinced that adherence to such principles will promote better strategy execution, make the company a better performer, and positively impact its reputation in the marketplace. To promote belonging, Airbnb developed processes for:

- Honest two-way communication;
- Screening applicants and hiring those who will mesh well with the culture; incorporating discussions of the company's culture and behavioral norms into recruiting, onboarding, and orientation of new employees;
- Having senior executives frequently reiterate the importance and role of company values and ethical principles at company events and in internal communications to employees;
- Using feedback from employee surveys to engage managers at all levels to be cultural role models and exhibit the advocated cultural norms in their own behaviors;
- Respecting diversity in observing holidays and key events in the company's evolution;
- Encouraging company personnel to exert strong peer pressure on co-workers to conform to expected cultural norms; and
- Promoting belonging by holding periodic ceremonies and events to recognize employees who excelled in displaying the company values and ethical principles.

End of Chapter Strategic Planning Exercise

Choosing an Employer

To seek out in identifying a prospective employer's culture? In answering this question, first take some time to do homework on a specific company's:

- Leadership and how that leader "sets the tone at the top";
- Defined spirit and character that pervade its work climate;
- Revered traditions and oft-repeated stories about "heroic acts" and "how we do things around here";

- Approaches to people management and the official policies, procedures, and operating practices that paint the white lines for the behavior of its personnel; and
- Shared values, business principles, and ethical standards that management preaches and practices.

Now, please explain in writing or in a short video clip which core values you would be *most unlikely* to put on your list, for example:

- Commitment to "ends justify the means" and "not invented here" approaches
- Winking at or casting a blind eye to unethical behavior
- Disintegrating teamwork and uncooperative attitudes
- Maintaining cut-throat competition with industry rivals, and
- Encouraging the formation of clashing subcultures to deter change and innovative ideas.

Further Reading

Abebe, M. A. (2009). Leadership characteristics of declining firms attempting turnaround: An empirical examination. *Journal of Strategy and Management, 2*(3), 201–216.

Anderson, C., & Gilinsky, A. (2022). Burbank housing: Building from the inside out. In A. A. Thompson, M. Peteraf, & J. E. Gamble, *Crafting & executing strategy, 23/e*. McGraw–Hill.

Boyd, D. P. (2011). Lessons from turnaround leaders. *Strategy and Leadership, 29*(3), 36–43.

Bovim, R. V. (2019). *How Airbnb became the world's best place to work*. @Living Room. Retrieved January 2, 2023. from: https://www.livingroomanalytics.com/how-airbnb-became-the-worlds-best-place-to-work

Covin, J., & Slevin, D. P. (1990). New venture strategic posture, structure, and performance: An industry life cycle analysis. *Journal of Business Venturing*, 5, 123–135.

Culture Amp. (n.d.). *How to foster belonging for all employees*. Retrieved August 12, 2021, from: https://www.cultureamp.com/resources/culture-first-on-demand-americas/how-do-we-best-foster-belonging-for-all-employees-feat-airbnb#main-content

Espinoza, N. (2020). *Opening La Texanita Restaurant 2?* MBA student course project for Sonoma State University, Spring 2020, used by written permission.

Levy, M. (2020, April 9). *Growth by design at Airbnb*. Speech to the HR Congress. Retrieved January 2, 2023, from https://www.youtube.com/watch?v=04VmcMUQoZs

Miles, R. E., & Snow, C. C. (1978). *Organizational strategy, structure, and process*. McGraw–Hill.

Miles, R. E., Snow, C. C., & Sharfman, L. (1993). Industry variety and firm performance. *Strategic Management Journal, 14*, 1–21.

Naman, J. L., & Slevin, D. S. (1993). Entrepreneurship and the concept of fit: A model and empirical tests. *Strategic Management Journal, 14*, 137–153.

Rosen, J., as quoted in Pichel, C., & Gilinsky, A. (1996). *Fantastic foods—1995 (case study)*.

Smith, L. (2020, October 17). 'Zoom towns' are exploding in the West. *Fast Company*. Retrieved October 24, 2020 from: https://www.fastcompany.com/90564796/zoom-towns-are-exploding-in-the-west. See also https://www.youtube.com/watch?v=YpR4re8oubw for a KSDK video report on the evolution of communities in St. Louis, MO into Zoom towns.

Stevenson, H. H., Roberts, M., & Grousbeck, H. (1989). *New business ventures and the entrepreneur*. Irwin.

Thomas, I. (2021, June 16). *How new UPS CEO Carol Tomé jumpstarted the stock after six years of going nowhere*. CNBC Evolve online. Retrieved November 11, 2021 from: https://www.cnbc.com/2021/06/16/how-new-ups-ceo-jumpstarted-stock-after-a-six-year-flat-line.html

Zeyssolff, C., Zeyssolff Winery, Alsace, France, personal interview with Dr. Coralie Haller, Ecole Management de Strasbourg and Dr. Armand Gilinsky, Sonoma State University, June 2020.

CHAPTER 3

Scanning the Environment

Abstract This chapter is concerned with diagnosing and analyzing industries and their environments as well as developing decision-making tools to prescribe strategies to gain a competitive advantage over rivals. We should consider the disparate needs and expectations of all stakeholders and how those needs may sometimes come into conflict. Consensus can often be difficult to achieve, especially during periods of great uncertainty or what strategists call turbulent environments.

Keywords Environmental scanning · Industry drivers · Key performance indicators · Opportunity scoping · Situation assessment · Strategy as practice

Assessing the Macro-Environment

In the previous chapter we examined strategic leadership styles and their impacts on a company's culture. This chapter takes up the issue of situation assessment, also known as scanning the environment, which is essentially an analysis of the macro-environment and given industry

A. Gilinsky, *Business Strategy for a Better Normal*,
https://doi.org/10.1007/978-3-031-28708-4_3

in which organizations operate. Tools for conducting the analysis and making decisions are also presented.

The core content of a strategy includes (Rumelt, 2011: 79):

1. Diagnosis of the situation at hand, that is, does it manifest stability and growth (opportunity-rich);
2. creation or identification of a guiding policy for dealing with critical difficulties in unfavorable environments (opportunity-poor); and
3. a set of coherent actions.

If new insights or ideas for strategic planning are not needed, deduction is sufficient.

There can be times when those results are fine, when no new opportunities seem to have developed, and no new risks have appeared. In those instances, the logical answer to the strategy question is simply, "Keep it up, do more of the same." In the vernacular, the conventional wisdom is stated as, "If it ain't broke, don't fix it."

Yet, just like one uses preventive maintenance to take care of an automobile, managers need to be proactive to keep their organizations running smoothly. Planning is a continual process involving inductive reasoning, particularly in a rapidly changing environment.

In a world of change and flux, "more of the same" or "If it ain't broke, don't fix it," is reactive instead of proactive and rarely leads to success. A strategy must have a diagnostic component, that is, a plan that embodies flexibility, incorporating some new ideas or insights with combinations of resources and opportunities (Rumelt, 2011: 244).

Opportunity-Rich or Opportunity-Poor?

Managers must analyze whether their operating macro-environment has numerous opportunities, i.e., "opportunity-rich," or whether the environment is mature or declining with slow or negative growth and minimal opportunities for innovation, i.e., "opportunity-poor."

Opportunity-rich environments. An example of an opportunity-rich environment is the segment of information technology known as software-as a-service (SaaS), which is a cloud delivery model in which software is centrally hosted and delivered and distributed to computers and mobile devices on a subscription basis. Spending on SaaS experienced the highest growth rate within the tech industry and is projected to grow further in 2021, offsetting the decline caused by the COVID-19 pandemic in 2020, according to Statista. Software-as a-service is opportunity-rich as it represents the fastest growing sector in the U.S. economy as of this writing. In 2020, Salesforce was the largest SaaS vendor worldwide with a market share of 9.3%. The three other key players in the market included Microsoft, SAP, and Google, so with four dominant rivals, SaaS is a highly concentrated industry.

Opportunity-poor environments. By contrast, the restaurant industry is considered to be opportunity-poor because the industry growth rate fell from a compounded annual increase of 2.5% from 2011 to 2018 to a negative 14% in 2020. The number of rivals in the U.S. restaurant industry exceeded 660,000 in 2020, according to Statista, indicating a highly fragmented industry.

Strategists have used innovation to transform companies that operate in opportunity-poor environments, characterized by mature industries with slow or negative growth prospects. Supermarkets and hotels were traditionally characterized as opportunity-poor with slowing growth, diminishing innovation, and an increasing concentration of rival firms. Nevertheless, strategists have found ways to revamp customer service, introducing food delivery services, touchless payment and check-out systems for both supermarkets and hotels, and keyless room entry in hotels and motels.

Some top management teams operating in opportunity-poor environments pursue cost reductions and consolidation via mergers and acquisitions to increase market share and raise barriers to entry. Amazon in supermarkets and Marriott International hotels have been outstanding examples of this strategy. Amazon purchased Whole Foods Markets in 2017 and overtook Walmart as the largest food retailer by sales volume in 2021. Marriott International purchased Starwood Properties in 2016 and Elegant Hotels in 2019, leapfrogging Hilton International and the Intercontinental Hotel Group (IHG) to become the world's largest hotel brand in terms of number of properties in 2022.

Other managers, perceiving the environment to be opportunity-rich, recognize entry barriers, and pursue new product/service introductions, by identifying and developing unoccupied or vacant niches, and/or via innovation. Witness the recent growth of entrepreneurial food delivery services such as GrubHub/Seamless, DoorDash, UberEats, and Caviar, for some leading examples.

Top managers with a particular set of operating philosophies and values may tend to adopt a particular approach to strategy formulation that is complementary to and consistent with their style(s). Some managers choose to avoid or ignore changes; others embrace it.

Figure 3.1 is an environmental scanning tool to help you identify whether your company is in an opportunity-rich or opportunity-poor situation.

Quadrants

A. **Opportunity-poor.** Organizations are in highly concentrated, low-growth industries, where capturing market share is critical.
B. **Opportunity-rich.** Organizations are in highly concentrated, high-growth industries and have at least a temporary monopoly via innovation or dominate a segment that others cannot or will not choose to enter.
C. **Opportunity-rich.** Organizations are in highly fragmented, high-growth industries where rivals are jockeying for position and no dominant leader has yet emerged.
D. **Opportunity-poor.** Organizations are in highly fragmented, low-growth industries—not a long-term viable position.

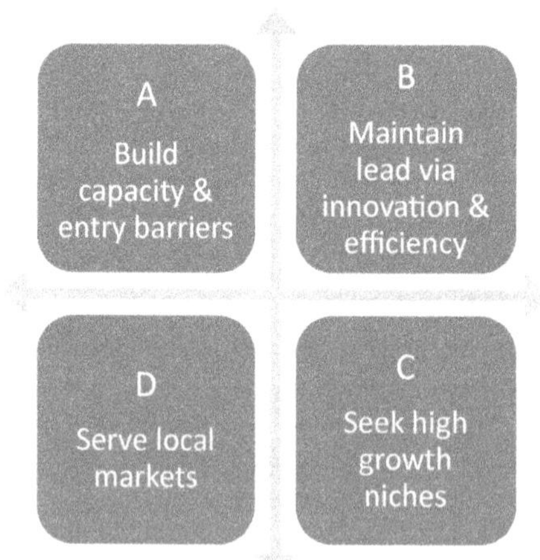

Fig. 3.1 Mapping strategic situations (*Source* Created by author)

The X-axis represents the degree of expected future industry growth, showing low or no growth on the left side, but high growth in excess of 10–20% on the right side. The Y-axis represents the degree of concentration or number of rivals in a given industry, showing many rivals or a highly fragmented industry on the bottom, and few rivals or a highly concentrated industry on the top.

Environments need to be continuously monitored and scanned for changes, since it is unlikely that the plan that worked yesterday will be effective in today's (or even tomorrow's) marketplace.

Leaders of organizations need to develop annual strategic plans that establish short-term (one year) as well as intermediate-term (three-to-five years) goals and objectives. Goals and objectives are typically based on acquiring and deploying specific resources, capabilities, and activities.

In addition to these short-term plans, leaders need to continually address the long-term perspective of the venture.

Typically, this involves setting **goals and objectives** (up to three)—and then identifying strategies (typically, three-to-five to attain each goal) and tactics (typically, three-to-five for each strategy) to support those—over a time horizon of five years or longer.

Strategic planning, like all other activities, is an iterative, dynamic process. Changes are made over time, as necessary, with the purpose of creating vibrant long-term health depending upon the company's situation.

Key Performance Indicators

Key Performance Indicators (KPIs) are used by strategists to benchmark the progress of their organizations toward achievement of stated objectives, such as profitability and growth.

Typically, a strategist monitors the health of a business via financial analysis and benchmarking the analyses against rivals. See Table 3.1 for typical KPIs.

A strategist's decisions, both wise and unwise, can play out in several ways when it comes to measuring results and benchmarking those against industry rivals or even industry averages. Results affect stakeholders: owners, investors, creditors, employees, suppliers, competitors, communities, unions, and the natural environment. However, measurement of non-financial metrics has historically been limited and often unconnected to an organization's strategies. To bridge this gap, Kaplan and Norton

Table 3.1 Examples of key performance indicators

Type of measure	*Calculation*	*Interpretation*	*Caveats*
Efficiency	Sales revenue = Price (of product) × Quantity sold or volume		May need to adjust for discounts and returns of merchandise
	Total costs = Costs of sales + other direct costs + Admin overhead		Some costs may vary with volume sold, and are known as variable costs
	Gross profit = Sales revenue ($) – Cost of sales	Gross margin = Gross profit/Sales, expressed as a percentage, also known as Economic Value Added Can be compared with other industries	Need to factor in other direct costs in making the product or performing the service
	Operating profit = Sales revenue ($) – Total costs ($)	Operating margin = Operating profit/sales, expressed as a percentage, also known as the cash-generating potential of a business Can be compared with other companies in an industry	May be distorted by non-cash expenses such as depreciation and amortization
	Net profit ($) = Sales revenue ($) – Total costs ($) – Taxes	Net margin or return on sales = Net profit/Sales, expressed as a percentage Can be compared with close rivals or companies of similar size and product/service lineup	Need to factor in Taxes = Federal + State + Local, which may be impacted by regulatory changes or legal form of business chosen

Type of measure	*Calculation*	*Interpretation*	*Caveats*
Growth	Annual rates of change in revenues and profits = (This year – Last year)/Last year Compound annual growth rates (CAGR) PV = first period, always entered as a negative number (or inverse of the actual number) FV = most recent period N = number of periods Assume no payments or other factors Solve for RATE (on Excel) or "I" (on a financial calculator)	Shows the year-on-year growth of a business	Masks longer-term trends
Cost to acquire a new customer	Sum of costs associated per new customer, which can include: advertising, marketing team, sales team, creative, technical, publishing, production Inventory upkeep, etc	Amount spent on marketing and sales) divided by customers acquired	
MRR or Monthly Recurring Revenue	Number of monthly subscribers * the average revenue per user (ARPU)	MRR is the predictable total revenue generated by your business from all the active subscriptions in a particular month. It includes recurring charges from discounts, coupons, and recurring add-ons, but excludes one-time fees. MRR can assess the present financial health of the business and project the future earnings based on the active subscriptions	Formula excludes all one-time, non-recurring payments; for instance, implementation or professional service fees, hardware, and discounts

(continued)

Table 3.1 (continued)

Type of measure	*Calculation*	*Interpretation*	*Caveats*
CLV or lifetime value of a customer	CLV applies the concept of the net present value (NPC) to cash flows attributed to the customer relationship PV = first period cash flows, always entered as a negative number (or inverse of the actual number) FV = most distant period cash flows N = number of periods I = Discount rate Assume no payments or other factors Solve for Net Present Value (NPV)	Customer value * average customer lifespan Customer lifetime value encourages firms to shift their focus from quarterly profits to the long-term health of their customer relationships, and involves: Forecasting remaining customer lifetime (most often in years) Forecasting future revenues (most often year-by-year), based on estimation about future products purchased and price paid Estimation of costs for delivering those products Calculation of the net present value of these future amounts	While CLV Is demonstrably **the** model for many successful e-commerce businesses, the future revenue streams as well customer time horizons are always a "best guess." CLV can be calculated in many ways. In the case of a subscription model, a simple method is to take the average monthly amount expected from each customer and divide it by your churn rate (the rate at which you lose customers each month)

Source Created by author

(2002) suggest the concept of the *Balanced Scorecard*—stakeholders associated with each segment of the organization should be thought of as partners. Each partner has expectations and needs.

Reaching a consensus on mission and vision, strategy, and key success factors is forged based on the beliefs, values, and needs of an organization's multiple stakeholders. Sometimes, however, consensus among stakeholders can be elusive, as will be discussed in Chapter 5.

Environmental Scanning Tools

Every company operates in a broad "macro-environment" that comprises six principal components. Each of these components has the potential to affect a company's industry and competitive environment:

1. Political factors,
2. Economic conditions in the firm's general environment (local, country, regional, worldwide),
3. Socio-cultural forces,
4. Technological factors,
5. Ecological or natural environment, and
6. Legal/regulatory conditions.

An analysis of the impact of these factors is often referred to as PESTEL Analysis, as shown in Table 3.2. PESTEL is an acronym that serves as a reminder of the six components involved.

Company managers continuously scan the external environment (sometimes called the task environment), remaining alert for potentially important developments, assessing their impact and influence, and adapting the company's direction and strategy as needed. However, the factors in a company's external environment having the biggest strategy-shaping impact typically pertain to the immediate industry and competitive environment (Andrews, 1980).

To illustrate, much of the growth of industries such as clothing retailers was previously fueled by the increasing number of women entering into the workforce between 1930 and 1970 (Bomey, 2020). But with pandemic-related layoffs and furloughs in 2020, school closures, and social distancing regulations, many women began to exit the workforce,

Table 3.2 Components of a PESTEL analysis

Macro-environmental force	*Examples*
Political	Any government intervention in the economy, including: tax, fiscal, and energy policies, and tariffs, the political climate, the federal banking system, bailouts, etc.
Economic	General economic circumstances that affect consumer confidence and discretionary income, including: interest, exchange, savings, and the unemployment rates, and inflation, the rate of economic growth, trade deficits or surpluses, per capita domestic product, and markets for stocks and bonds
Socio-cultural	Societal values, attitudes, cultural factors, lifestyles, health, demographics such as the population size, growth rate, and age and income distribution
Technological	The pace of technical developments that have the potential for wide-ranging effects on society, such as genetic engineering and nanotechnology, institutional entities such as research and development (R&D) consortia, university-sponsored technology incubators, and government control over the Internet
Environmental	Weather, natural disasters, climate change, water shortages, all factors that directly impact industries such as insurance, farming, energy production, and tourism
Legal & Regulatory	Consumer safety, labor, antitrust, occupational health and safety, banking regulation, patent and copyright laws, immigration policies, and minimum wage legislation

Source Prepared by author of this textbook

causing spending on clothing to markedly decline in the short-term (Cain & Stone, 2020).

Top management has the obligation and opportunity to scan the firm's environment and identify issues of strategic importance to an organization. Table 3.3 is an example of a PESTEL Analysis Table regarding Ikea's entry into China. A PESTEL analysis can be useful to summarize, describe, and evaluate the most important forces that emerge from an environmental scan. This analysis can also illustrate how change might impact the key industry drivers.

While macro-environmental forces impact all firms within an industry, some manage to prosper by attaining a competitive advantage among their industry rivals by staking out either a lowest cost (in mass markets

Table 3.3 Rating the importance of external strategic factors for IKEA in China

Macro-environmental force	*Chinese home furnishings industry*	*Potential impact on IKEA in China*
Political	+/+ • Import policies and tariffs • Inward investment and JV policies • Bureaucratic "wait-states"	++
Economic	++ • Projected changes in per capita income • Country debt • Inflation and currency exchange rates • Labor costs	++
Socio-cultural	++ • Chinese culture and values • Consumer attitudes and preferences • Level of home ownership • Demographic projections	++
Technological	+ • New product innovation • Social media usage • E-commerce	+
Ecological	+/− • Sustainable sourcing of lumber • Catastrophic weather events	+/−
Legal/regulatory	+/− • China labor law • Patent protection laws • Urban and suburban zoning laws	+/−

KEY:
++ = Strong impact
+ = Moderate impact
+/− = Possible impact
Source Prepared by author of this textbook

or focused market segments) or differentiated (again, in mass markets or focused segments or niches) position. There can be *only one* lowest cost leader in an industry, such as Walmart in retail or Southwest Airlines in passenger aviation, but there may also be numerous differentiated rivals. By contrast, the wine industry is considered a purely competitive industry, in that there are many rivals—over 11,000 wineries in the U.S. alone—that are seeking unique positions based on *terroir* (location, soil, and climate), quality due to the skill of the winemaker, or the company's history. There is no recognizable lowest cost leader, so all firms in that industry must try to differentiate (Adams, 2021).

Driving Forces

Industry and competitive conditions frequently change because forces are enticing or pressuring stakeholders (e.g., competitors, customers, suppliers) to alter their actions in important ways. The most powerful of the change agents are called *driving forces* (sometimes known as "industry drivers") because these collectively have the greatest impact in reshaping an industry landscape and altering competitive conditions within that industry.

Some driving forces originate in a company's macro-environment; others originate in the company's more immediate industry and competitive environment.

Driving forces analysis. This involves three steps:

1. Identify what the driving forces are;
2. Assess whether the drivers of change are, on the whole, acting to make the industry more or less attractive; and
3. Determine what strategic changes are needed in order to prepare for and mitigate the impact of the driving forces.

Examples of driving forces in an industry may include:

Increasing globalization that occurs when industry members begin seeking out customers in foreign markets or when production activities begin to migrate to countries where costs are lowest. The scope of competition then begins to shift from primarily a regional or national focus to an international or global focus.

Changes in who buys the product and how they use it, caused by shifts in buyer demographics and the ways products or services are used that can greatly alter industry and competitive conditions.

Changes in industry leadership that may result in a much-changed competitive landscape, irrespective of whether industry growth rises or falls. The changing of the guard in terms of industry leadership, e.g., in market share, standards, or innovation, always disrupts the status quo.

Emerging new Internet and big data capabilities and applications enabling companies to reach new consumer segments increases the number of rivals a company faces and often escalates rivalry by pitting pure online sellers against brick-and-mortar sellers.

Technological change and manufacturing process innovation that can cause disruptive change in an industry by introducing substitutes that offer buyers an irresistible price/performance combination, or alter the industry landscape by opening up whole new industry frontiers.

Entry or exit of major rivals that often produces a changed competitive landscape, not only with new key players but also with new rules for competing. Similarly, exit of a major firm changes the competitive structure by reducing the number of market leaders and increasing the dominance of the leaders who remain.

Product/marketing innovation(s), that tend(s) to alter the pattern of competition in an industry by attracting more first-time buyers, rejuvenating industry growth, and/or increasing product differentiation, with concomitant effects on rivalry, entry threat, and buyer power.

Diffusion of technical know-how across companies and countries about how to perform a particular activity or execute a particular manufacturing technology—can occur through scientific journals, trade publications, onsite plant tours, word of mouth among suppliers and customers, employee migration, and Internet sources. As knowledge spreads, highly differentiated products tend to evolve into commodity goods.

Changes in cost and efficiency that widen or shrink differences in the costs among key rivals in an industry, cost structures that tend to dramatically alter the state of competition, e.g., iPads, Kindles, and eBooks, which cost less to produce and distribute than print books.

Fluctuations in uncertainty and business risk that may deter outsiders from entering an industry, and make incumbents more cautious about making aggressive capital investments to expand, which may be compounded in foreign markets where demand is just emerging or where political conditions are volatile.

Changes in the long-term industry growth rate that can affect the balance between industry supply and buyer demand, entry and exit, and the character and strength of competition.

Emerging societal concerns, attitudes, and lifestyles that may involve changing attitudes, values, and beliefs toward climate change, use of synthetic additives or GMOs, health and longevity, or social problems such as crime, homelessness, drug addiction, and race relations.

Regulatory influences and government policy changes that often mandate significant alterations of industry practices and strategic approaches; foreign governments can drive competitive changes by opening their domestic markets to foreign participation or closing them to protect domestic companies.

That there are so many different potential drivers of change explains why a full understanding of all types of change drivers is a fundamental part of analyzing industry dynamics. In a particular industry, however, no more than three or four of these drivers are likely to be powerful enough to qualify as the major determinants of why and how an industry's competitive conditions are changing. Our task as strategists is to carefully evaluate the forces of industry and competitive change to separate the major drivers from the minor ones.

Thus, the most important steps in conducting driving forces analysis are to determine whether the collective impact of the driving forces will be to increase or decrease market demand, make competition more or less intense, and lead to higher or lower industry profitability. A company's foreseen capability to achieve and sustain profitability is, after all, what makes an industry attractive to enter. We will take up this issue in greater detail in Chapter 4.

Strategy as Practice

Strategic change actually is a dynamically a strategy is composed of specific actions, interactions of practitioners, and the flow of activities, which exert powerful influences on ultimate performance outcomes (Sarasvathy, 2001).

Observing the concrete actions and practices that underlie the numerous processes that companies perform is critical for understanding the success or failure of strategic change. In response to environmental variations, companies should generate strategic alternatives by using the feedback from experimentation and iterative learning, to see if any will fly (Wei & Zhang, 2020).

Will the Strategy Fly?

Emily Dickinson, a mid-nineteenth-century American poet, once wrote that "'Hope' is the thing with feathers that perches in the soul." For hope to fly, leaders need to be mindful of promising opportunities and possess the willingness to learn continuously.

Some researchers have studied family firms in which the CEOs report high levels of expected well-being after retirement have higher levels of overall performance (Collins et al., 2016). Collins and his team report that, CEOs who have a positive outlook regarding their upcoming retirement likely have a more positive outlook in general, more willing to pursue opportunities, embrace input from others in the organization, and increasingly empower their employees to make relevant decisions for the organization. Each of these characteristics can improve the quality of decision-making in a firm and positively impact firm performance.

In a recent case study about an Irish manufacturing firm, Glennon Brothers (2017), Clinton and his co-authors observe:

> Over the many years that Pat and Mike had worked together [at the Glennon Brothers' sawmill], they had developed similar mannerisms. At this point, they both scratched their balding heads as they looked first at the whiteboard and then at the Murphy & Sons headline that lay strewn on the office table. In reality, they knew that there was no time to procrastinate—their legacy was effectively in the balance. The "elephant in the room" remained the knowledge that they needed to move from being managers to managing managers. But how do old dogs learn new tricks?

Frazier (2018) recounts a story told to him by Jordan Temkin, a world champion racer of drones powered by electric motors and batteries:

> "When we started flying, we could hardly do anything," Temkin told me in Fort Collins last fall. "I built my first drone from a frame pattern I found online and printed out on my 3-D printer. I ordered parts for it and put it together and just started flying. I loved it, but I crashed all the time. Today, we can do moves we couldn't have even thought of two years ago. That's partly because the technology kept getting better and partly because our skills improved."

Thus, if you and your organization are intending to grow, before using any of the tools described in this chapter, first consider carefully how to instill positive thinking and continuous learning.

End of Chapter Mini-Case: Robinhood Markets, Inc.

Armand Gilinsky

Vlad Tenev and Baiju Bhatt, the Robinhood Markets Inc. co-founders who drew a generation of young people into investing on their phones using an app, officially became billionaires upon the company's initial public offering (IPO) in late July 2021. Robinhood was a popular online trading site, and the company sold shares to the public on July 29, 2021 (ticker symbol: HOOD) for $38 apiece, which put the estimated net worth of Tenev, the company's chief executive officer, at $2.4 billion, according to the Bloomberg Billionaires Index. Bhatt, who had shared the company CEO duties until 2020, was then worth $2.8 billion. Robinhood later announced on August 21, 2021 that it planned to give away $100,000 to recruit new investors: $500 away to 200 users who join or refer friends to the site by September 16, 2021.

Robinhood competed in the investment banking and securities dealing sector of the financial services industry. According to an August 2021 report by Derek Longhini in *IBISWorld*, the US investment banking and securities dealing sector had grown by an annual compound rate of 4.5% from 2016 to 2021, and was valued at nearly $138 billion in 2021. Major rivals in the sector included Bank of America, Citigroup, Goldman Sachs, JP Morgan Chase, and Morgan Stanley. Altogether, these five companies owned an 81.1% market share.

Downside Risks

Robinhood reported a $501.7 million, or $2.16 per share loss on August 18, 2021 for the second quarter. The company has previously enticed new traders to join by giving away a share of stock to various other publicly

A. Gilinsky
Sonoma State University, Rohnert Park, CA, USA

traded companies. Cryptocurrencies made up 41% of all of Robinhood's $565.3 million in revenue in the second quarter of 2021, up from 17% in the first three months of the year and from just three percent at the start of 2020. Cryptocurrencies increased to $233 million in the second quarter of 2021, compared to $5 million in the second quarter of 2020.

Critics have contended that Robinhood's site engaged in gamification, using bright colors and congratulatory messages that can encourage impulsive and emotional investing behavior. In a well-publicized tragedy reported by Robert Neal in *American Banker*, Alex Kearns, a 20-year-old investor who had a negative balance of $730,000 on his account, committed suicide in 2020. In a suicide note shared on Twitter by his family, Kearns asked why "a 20-year-old with no income" was able to get nearly $1 million worth of leverage. "There was no intention to be assigned this much and take this much risk, and I only thought that I was risking the money that I actually owned," Kearns said in the post, adding that he had "no clue" what he was doing. The case was investigated by the U.S. Senate's Finance Committee in 2020, and lawmakers at that time called Kearns's death "heartbreaking" and "highly alarming" in a letter sent to the company.

Responses to Critics

Robinhood altered some of its prior practices that drew criticism, for example, it no longer allowed minors to trade as all of its investors must be 18 years or older. The company was fined $70 million during 2021 over outages and misleading and exposing customers to risky trading tools. The firm approved thousands of customers for options trading, but those customers did not satisfy the firm's eligibility criteria, according to federal regulators.

According to a survey that the company commissioned in 2020, Robinhood's customers were still younger than the industry norm, with a median age of 31; 70% were millennials or Gen-Z. They were also more ethnically diverse: 60% of their customers were white, compared with 78% at other brokerages. Nineteen percent of Robinhood users were Hispanic, 10% are Asian, and nine percent are Black—figures close to the makeup of the U.S. as a whole, although women remained underrepresented at Robinhood and its rivals, accounting for about a third of customers.

Uncertain Outlook

The likelihood of Robinhood turning those traders into profit-generating, long-term customers appeared to be uncertain—especially given the incumbency and deep pockets of its competitors. In an interview with *Fortune* in late 2020, Joe Grundfest, a Stanford Law School professor and former SEC commissioner who knew Tenev and Bhatt, said such skepticism underestimates the power of a true innovator. "By that logic, Walmart should be kicking Amazon's ass, CBS should be wiping the floor with Netflix, GM should be kicking the corn out of Tesla," he says.

The Robinhood app, which initially was intended as a community for stock picking and investment advice, later morphed into a trading platform. They developed the idea after seeing the Occupy Wall Street protests in New York's Zuccotti Park in 2011 and wanted to help introduce more people to investing. Tenev had said in a 2016 interview that his wife, Celina, accidentally came up with the company's name when trying to explain what Bhatt and her husband were up to: "'They're in finance, but they're not investment bankers or traders or anything like that. They are the Robin Hood of finance."

As of late summer 2021, according to *Bloomberg News*, 17.7 million people were using the Robinhood app each month, more than half of which were first-time investors.

Lessons learned. While opportunity-rich markets may offer a high upside potential for entrants, accompanying every opportunity there are challenges involved. Innovative strategies can not only open up new markets, but also result in unintended consequences.

End of Chapter Strategic Planning Exercise

Scoping an Opportunity

A friend or family member has asked you for career advice. Which industry or sector would you recommend that this person avoid? Which industry or sector is most promising in terms of opportunity? That is, which career path is opportunity-poor, and which is opportunity-rich?

You may need to do some research. Depending upon your access to your university's library, a good place to start is to look at the electronic business research databases such as Business Source Premier, IBISWorld, Mergent Online, or Statista.

Further Reading

Adams, A. (2021, February). Review of the industry: State of distribution. *Wine Business Monthly*, 70–71.

Andrews, K. R. (1980). *The concept of corporate strategy* (2nd ed.). Richard D. Irwin.

Anon. (2020, February 5). Was Instagram the steal of the century? *The New York Times online*. https://www.nytimes.com/2020/02/05/business/dealbook/instagram-20-billion-revenue.html. Accessed February 8, 2020

Bomey, N. (2020, September 9). Mall owners Simon and Brookfield to acquire J.C. Penney out of bankruptcy despite 'screaming matches.' *USA Today online*. https://www.usatoday.com/story/money/2020/09/09/jcpenney-sale-simon-property-group-brookfield-property-partners/5761731002/. Accessed September 13, 2020.

Cain, A., & Stone, M. (2020, August 25). *These 31 retailers and restaurant companies have filed for bankruptcy or liquidation in 2020*. Business Insider.com. https://www.businessinsider.com/retailers-filed-bankruptcy-liquidation-closing-stores-2020-2#neiman-marcus-filed-for-chapter-11-bankruptcy-on-may-7-citing-inexorable-pressure-from-the-coronavirus-pandemic-11. Accessed August 31, 2020.

Clinton, E., Faherty C. M., Diaz-Moriana, V., & Craig, J. B. (2017, May) Glennon Brothers: Old dogs need to learn new tricks. *Entrepreneurship: Theory & Practice*, 455–468.

Collins, J. D., Worthington, W. J., & Schoen, J. E. (2016). Family business CEO succession: Examining personal retirement expectations. *Journal of Small Business Strategy, 26*(2), 51–70.

Duncan, R. B. (1972). Characteristics of organizational environments and perceived environmental uncertainty. *Administrative Science Quarterly, 17*, 313–327.

Frazier, I. (2018, February 5). The trippy, high-speed world of drone racing. *The New Yorker*.

Kaplan, R. S., & Norton, D. P. (2002). *Partnering and the balanced scorecard, working knowledge*. Harvard Business School.

Longhini, D. (2021, August). *Investment banking and securities dealing in the US: US Industry (NAICS) Report 52311*. IBISWorld.

Melin, A. (2021, July 29). *Robinhood duo ride trading frenzy to billionaire riches*. Bloomberg.Com, N.PAG.

Neal, R. W. (2020). Lawmakers grill Robinhood following 20-year-old trader's suicide. *American Banker, 185*(138), 1.

Roberts, J. J. (2020). Stealing (market share) from the rich. *Fortune, 182*(4), 102–108.

Rumelt, R. (2011). *Good strategy bad strategy: The difference and why it matters*. Crown Business.

Sarasvathy, S. D. (2001). Causation and effectuation: Toward a theoretical shift from economic inevitability to entrepreneurial contingency. *Academy of Management Review, 26*(2), 243–263.

Statista. (2021a). *Restaurant Industry in the US*. Report #did-11721-1.

Statista. (2021b). *Software as a Service (SaaS),* Report #did-31317-1.

Wei, Z., & Zhang, L. (2020). How to perform strategic change? A strategy as practice perspective. *Chinese Management Studies, 14*(3), 811–832.

Wu, T. (2020, July 5). Better buyouts. *The New York Times*, SR 10. Retrieved July 5, 2020 from https://www.nytimes.com/2020/06/30/opinion/sunday/mergers-buyouts-economy-inequality.html?searchResultPosition=2

CHAPTER 4

Industry Attractiveness

Abstract This chapter is concerned with diagnosing industry forces and key success factors (KSF). You will learn how to use Ansoff and TOWS matrices to generate strategic alternatives for competing successfully against the power of the industry forces and positioning your business to meet or exceed your industry's KSF.

Keywords Ansoff matrix · Competitive forces · Diversification · Key success factors · TOWS matrix

The Power of Competitive Forces

Choosing *where* to compete is as important for organizations as choosing *how* to compete.

How do we know whether or not an industry is attractive? Let's begin by examining the competitive forces.

Michael E. Porter's (1979, 1980, 2008) "Five Forces" conceptual framework assesses industry attractiveness and factors influencing competitor power. It is based on the implicit assumption that an industry can be defined as any number of firms producing and marketing products or developing and delivering services which can be considered "close substitutes" for one another. These forces include:

A. Gilinsky, *Business Strategy for a Better Normal*,
https://doi.org/10.1007/978-3-031-28708-4_4

1. The intensity of competitive rivalry among sellers, which is driven by...
2. the threat of entry of new competitors,
3. the threat of substitute products from other industries,
4. the degree of supplier bargaining power, and
5. the degree of buyer bargaining power.

Now, fellow strategists, let's apply and rate these five forces for the U.S. domestic wine industry. Let's use a rating system to assess the five forces. We typically use stars (★) and half stars (1/2★). A five-star (★★★★★) industry is considered very attractive. Industries with fewer than two stars (★★) are unattractive; that is, firms have great difficulty generating above-average ROIs. In Table 4.1 we can see an example that applies a ratings system to the Porter's Five-Forces analysis:

To take a deeper dive into Table 4.1.

Rivalry Among Competing Sellers: Moderate to High

Rivalry in the premium wine industry is increasing because of the proliferation of domestic and international wine brands available for purchase at both on-premises (hotels, airlines, restaurants) and off-premises (specialty wine shops, supermarkets and hypermarkets, grocery stores, and direct sales via tasting rooms and the Internet) points-of-sale. The cost to switch brands for trade intermediates and consumers is low. Customers have a wide spectrum of *appellations of origin*, *varietals*, and brand choices from which to choose. The U.S. wine industry is composed of approximately 11,000+ wineries and the top 50 wineries account for 90% of U.S. domestic production as of early 2021, according to *Wine Business Monthly* (Penn, 2021a). Imports from "New World" wine producers, such as Australia and New Zealand, increase competition. The U.S. wine industry is highly regulated: prohibiting direct sales to consumers in all but 13 states.

Outside the U.S., import restrictions to protect domestic producers and tariffs deter U.S. producers' entry into export markets. Building knowledge of export markets' legal, distribution, and trade channels takes time and is costly.

Conglomerate corporations like Constellation Brands and Gallo increase rivalry by purchasing brands and leveraging their access to

Table 4.1 Rating industry attractiveness using Porter's (2008) five-forces analysis

Force	*Rating Key*	*Evaluation*	*Number of stars*
Threat of New Entrants	★ = low threat (high barriers) 1/2★ = moderate	Economies of scale—Moderate Product differentiation —Low/Moderate Capital requirements—High Brand identity—Moderate Absolute cost advantages—High Access to distribution—High	★ Low threat (high barriers)
Threat of Substitutes	★ = low threat (zero substitutes) 1/2★ = moderate	Price-performance—Moderate Switching costs—Moderate Propensity to substitute—Moderate	1/2★ Moderate
Bargaining Power of Customers	★ = low power 1/2★ = moderate	Product choices—Few Bargaining leverage—Low Low switching cost—Moderate Buyer information—Low Price sensitivity—Low Brand loyalty—Low/Moderate	★ Low (at least temporarily)
Bargaining Power of Suppliers	★ = low power 1/2★ = moderate	Industry importance—High Differentiation of inputs—Moderate Supplier concentration—Moderate Forward integration—Low Switching cost—Low/Moderate	1/2★ Moderate
Intensity of Firm Rivalry	★ = low intensity 1/2★ = moderate	Number of players—Low Growth rates—High Brand identity—Moderate Product similarity—Low/Moderate Exit barriers—High	1/2★ Moderate
Overall Evaluation of Industry Attractiveness		**ROI and profit potential are high**	**★★★ 1/2 ★ Moderately attractive, at best**

Source: Adapted by author for this book from Porter, M. E. (2008). The five competitive forces that shape strategy. *Harvard Business Review*, January, 79–93

distribution channels to make them viable market contenders. On the other hand, smaller wineries can create a surge in demand through quality control and limited release of high-end, high-priced labels.

Threat of Entry of New Competitors: Moderate to Low

There is a moderate-to-low entry threat of new competitors due to increasing barriers to entry: these may include capital intensity and government regulation. In addition, access to distribution is restricted (via the "three-tier" distribution system, which is consolidating).

In this environment, the only way for companies to grow market share is to take it away from a competitor, which intensifies rivalry.

Mobility and exit barriers are also increasing due to the high multiples paid for acquiring wineries, the limited re-usability of wine-making equipment for other purposes, and in some cases, a long family history of involvement with a particular brand.

Threat of Substitute Products: Moderate to High

Numerous substitute products compete with wine for the "dinner table segment" of beverages.

Direct substitutes include alcoholic beverages from numerous varieties of beers to spirits.

Indirect substitutes include non-alcoholic beverages that compete with wine such as carbonated drinks, water, juices, flavored non-carbonated drinks, teas and coffees, Cannabis, and other mood-altering substances are also indirect substitutes.

Direct and indirect beverage substitutes together create more intense competitive pressure, since both trade intermediates and end-consumers have so many available choices. For the serious wine-lover ("oenophile"), however, there is, of course, no substitute for wine.

Supplier Bargaining Power and Supplier-Seller Collaboration: Moderate

The competitive pressures are moderate from suppliers—grape growers—because although they have the ability to give larger customers a competitive advantage, grape supply is abundant relative to demand.

Large conglomerates that have a portfolio of many brands in the wine industry as well as large volumes of case production are able to leverage their buying power of raw materials: grapes and grape juice. This is accomplished via: (1) vertical integration into ownership of vineyards, (2) volume purchases from growers, and (3) capability to balance long-term contracts with growers with purchases on the spot market as growing conditions and harvest yields change. This, in turn, lowers their cost of goods, increases economies of scale, and places smaller competitors at a relative disadvantage.

Buyer Bargaining Power and Seller–Buyer Collaboration: Trade—High; Consumer—High

In the wine industry, trade intermediates have increasing clout due to consolidation of distribution channels. Consolidation among distribution and retail channels has augured dramatic changes in the wine industry.

The biggest news for wine distributors over the past decade was the number of consolidations of the industry's largest wholesalers. According to the February 2021 Annual Review of the Wine Industry in *Wine Business Monthly*, the top two distributors, Glazer's Wine & Spirits and RNDC Young's Market Co. attained control of more than half the total sales of domestic wine among U.S. consumers (Penn, 2021b).

That more and more wine is now sold through supermarkets has also worked in favor of well-known wines. Large wine conglomerates, such as Treasury Wine Estates, can now promise to supply a range of branded wines in sufficient quantities to supply entire supermarket chains. Simultaneously, consolidation of the U.S. retail industry is being driven by Amazon in the high end with Whole Foods, as well as by discount retailers such as Costco, WalMart, and Trader Joe's. Intermediates have the ability to choose brands to sell with extreme selectivity. The intermediates' goals are to have quick turnover, generate the highest possible margin, and not to necessarily carry the most prestige brands. Specialty store intermediates (that hold 23% of all wine sales) tend to have more influence on selecting higher-margin, prestige brands since their customers are more educated and wine oriented. Switching costs are very low, prompting trade buyers to seek the most profitable and fastest-selling brands.

The increasing role of mergers and acquisitions in the wine industry signals that: (a) the wine industry has evolved into a two-tier industry: few producers (highly concentrated) at the low end, and many producers (highly fragmented) at the premium end, and (b) the game for the larger premium wineries is beginning to change, from protecting a niche in a highly fragmented growth market to capturing greater share of a rapidly consolidating and maturing market.

The wine industry has become a two-tier market: premium-priced or low-end-(or economy) priced. Relative to the low-end segment, the premium segment of the wine industry remains attractive due to above-average growth rates and fragmentation. The "five forces" analysis indicates that on the whole, attractiveness of the premium wine segment remains high, although costs of entry are increasing. Conflicting needs for brand power and brand differentiation also restrict access to retail and on-premises markets. The low-end segment is unattractive due to flat sales and intense competition for market share from the major producers, such as E & J Gallo, JFJ Bronco ("Two-buck chuck"), Treasury Wine Estates, and The Wine Group.

Decision-Making Tools

SWOT and TOWS analyses. Most of us are probably more familiar with Kenneth Andrews' (1980) Strengths-Weaknesses-Opportunities-Threats (SWOT) analysis. SWOT analysis is considered by many strategy scholars to be the classic 2×2 matrix, but most people use it incorrectly. The trick with using SWOT analysis is, one needs to go beyond making lists in boxes and try and come up with strategic options that can be derived from analysis of:

1. **SO strategies**: Building on Strengths to take advantage of Opportunities;
2. **ST strategies**: Building on Strengths to deter Threats;
3. **WO strategies**: Shoring up Weaknesses to take advantage of Opportunities; and
4. **WT strategies**: Shoring up Weaknesses to minimize the impact of Threats

This variation is known as a Threats-Opportunities-Weaknesses-Strengths or **TOWS analysis.**

Ansoff's Product-Market Matrix. However, in all probability, the seminal model for strategic decision-making with respect to determining growth strategies is Ansoff's Product-Market "2×2" matrix, shown in Fig. 4.1. Ansoff's model denotes the two most essential strategy "levers" for any business: (1) the product or service it delivers and (2) the markets it sells into.

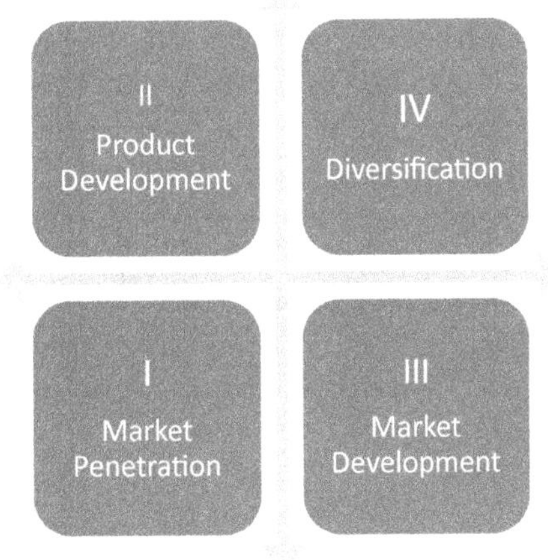

Fig. 4.1 Ansoff's Product-Market "2×2" Matrix (*Source* Ansoff, H. I. (1965). *Corporate Strategy*. New York: McGraw-Hill)

For each of these, there are two basic states: current and new. There are today's customers—and there is the rest of the world that *could* become customers. Businesses can sell more of their current offerings or they can modify them. By combining these two sets of possibilities, businesses can effectively model strategic choices in a manner that is both instructive for analysis and decision-making and easy to communicate to others.

Key

I. **Market penetration:** the easiest and first choice is to sell more of the same product or service to existing customers.

II. **Product development:** a company can sell new products or services to satisfied and loyal customers, drawing on the trust that has been established and their understanding of the needs and preferences of the customer group.

III. **Market development:** when a new product or service has been received warmly and there is lots of demand left to tap; when a product or service has proven its value in one market, the most natural thing to do is introduce it elsewhere, exploiting experience and testimonials from the last market.

IV. **Diversification***:* also known as business development, which should be applied with **great caution**, and generally only when none of the other three alternatives is available. Cost and risk tend to be higher when *both* a product or service is not only unproven but also the prospective market remains unknown.

Remember, Andrew's SWOT and Ansoff's Diversification matrices are conceptual frameworks that are generally *descriptive* of a firm's performance rather than *prescriptive*.

Instead, let's consider two prescriptive approaches—those that share a positive outlook and continuous learning. These are tools for assessing the key success factors for organizations in an industry and the diversification choices made to achieve success.

Key Success Factors

Competitive rivalry in any industry increases and becomes a stronger force when:

- Buyer demand is growing slowly;
- Buyer costs to switch brands are low;
- Products of industry members are commodities or else weakly differentiated;
- Firms in the industry have excess production capacity and/or inventory;
- Firms in the industry have high fixed costs or high storage costs;
- Competitors are numerous or are of roughly equal size and competitive strength;
- Rivals have diverse objectives, strategies, and/or countries of origin; and
- Rivals have emotional stakes in the business or face high exit barriers.

An industry's KSF are those competitive factors that most affect industry members' ability to survive and prosper in the marketplace: the particular strategy elements, product attributes, operational approaches, resources, and competitive capabilities that spell the difference between being a strong competitor and a weak competitor—and between profit and loss.

Regardless of the circumstances, an industry's KSF can always be deduced by asking the same three questions:

1. On what basis do buyers of the industry's product choose between the competing brands of sellers? That is, what product attributes and service characteristics are crucial?
2. Given the nature of competitive rivalry prevailing in the marketplace, what resources and competitive capabilities must a company have to be competitively successful?
3. What shortcomings are almost certain to put a company at a significant competitive disadvantage?

The benefit of doing all of these assessments is to assess how your organization ranks relative to rivals on each of the important factors, those KSF that determine market success and ascertain whether an organization has a proven competitive advantage or disadvantage vis-à-vis its key rivals.

Creating shareholder value. Shareholder value is created when a business earns a return on invested capital that exceeds its cost of capital. Generally speaking, the greater the spread between return on capital and cost of capital, the greater the shareholder value that is created. However, the spread may be magnified by growth. In other words, a high-growth business that has a low to moderate spread may create more shareholder value than a low-growth business that has a higher spread. Thus, executives and shareholders focus both on profitability and growth.

Ameer and Othman's (2012) investigation of the top 100 sustainable global companies in 2008, selected from a universe of 3,000 firms from the developed countries and emerging markets, found significant higher mean sales growth, returns on assets, profits before taxation, and cash flows from operations compared to the control companies (over the period of 2006–2010).

How is it that some businesses (and non-profit organizations) are able to find this "sweet spot" of growth and sustainability and others are not? Would diversification into other, potentially more attractive and profitable industries be a ticket to ride? The answer is rarely. One of the most challenging decisions a company can confront is whether to diversify, either in terms of line of business or its customer base. Surely, that decision typically depends on the situation or context (Markides, 1997).

Diversification Winners and Losers

For some embryonic industries or industry segments, planning for the next big thing is vital, as investors in early-stage companies want to see that the entrepreneurs have carefully planned a clear long-term growth trajectory and an opportunity to capture the lion's share of a growth market.

Probable winners. Uber's purchase of Postmates for about $2.6 billion on June 29, 2020 appeared to be a sure bet. One business report noted that a tie-up could bolster Uber's delivery business, Uber Eats, and help it compensate for the cratering of its core ride-hailing business, which collapsed in many cities because of the coronavirus pandemic. The on-demand food delivery market had consolidated, and Uber sought for new ways to make money. Food delivery services had yet to reach profitability, however, demand for those services had soared while restaurants were closed and people were either voluntarily or involuntarily staying at home (Isaac & Griffith, 2020).

That same day, June 29, 2020, Lululemon, the purveyor of expensive athleisure and activewear, announced that it was betting on the future of personalized remote exercise as a way to reach customers by acquiring Mirror, a home fitness start-up that marketed and sold a $1,495 wall-mounted mirror-like screen for streaming workout classes. The value of that deal was an estimated $500 million. This transaction promised to be a jackpot for Mirror's investors and its founding chief executive, Brynn Putnam, a former New York City Ballet dancer, who started the company in 2018 and had raised $72 million from investors. Mirror charged customers $39 a month to stream its live or on-demand classes. The purchase was said by observers to fit with Lululemon's ambitions to become an experiential brand and also add Mirror's revenue streams to those of Lululemon's (Masheshwari, 2020).

Even in relatively attractive industries, incumbent businesses always should be searching for future customer-market growth segments or developing innovative advances to the core product/service portfolio. That way, they can build some daylight between them and the "upstarts"—newer entrants (fast followers or late followers)—that are seeking to grab a share of the original product-service market. We can see this already occurring to some extent in the microbrewery industry. As industries mature and become saturated with rivals, a core business may become less profitable and/or stagnant and induce management to begin a search for newer, more profitable customer-markets in order to get back on a growth track and reward investors.

Probable losers. At other times, particularly during industry downturns, as a result of societal shocks like the COVID-19 pandemic, or in the face of global recessions, when most rivals are struggling, a company with financial "deep pockets" (or with access to same) can sometimes swoop in and purchase undervalued assets at bargain prices. Ascena Retail Group, which today operates some 3,900 stores in the U.S., Puerto Rico, and Canada, did precisely this in 2012, when it added Charming Shoppes to its portfolio of specialty retail stores that at that time included Lane Bryant, Dress Barn, Justice, Loft, and Catherine's. Ascena filed for bankruptcy in July 2020 with more than $1 billion in debt and plans to close many of its stores. The company's brands, including Ann Taylor, Lane Bryant, and Loft, were later sold to private equity firm Sycamore Partners.

Hanging in the balance. Diversifying lines of business or entry into new customer segments or seeking new markets is an unpredictable, high-stakes game because companies usually explore the decision in an atmosphere that is not conducive to thoughtful deliberation. Crafting strategies for the better normal can be analogous to walking a tightrope, only without a safety net underneath.

Diversification tests. In 1985, Michael E. Porter introduced three (3) tests for successful diversification based on the likelihood of increasing shareholder value (cf. Porter, 1985). These tests are:

1. *Industry attractiveness* (based on a five-force analysis),
2. *Cost-of-entry* (comparing costs of build v. buy), and
3. *Synergy or better-off* (will 1 + 1 = 3, in terms of customer knowledge, access to markets, competitive advantage, etc.?).

To complicate matters, diversification as a strategy regularly goes in and out of vogue. There is little conventional wisdom to guide managers as they consider a move that could greatly increase shareholder value or seriously damage it.

Research suggests, however, that if managers consider three questions, they can reduce the gamble of diversification. These questions include:

1. What can our company do better than any of our competitors in its current market?
2. What strategic assets do we need in order to succeed in the new market?
3. Can we catch up to or leapfrog competitors at their own game?

The issues that the questions raise, and the discussions they provoke, are typically heightened by the detailed financial analysis that is usually conducted *before* a diversification decision is made (Morgenson, 2016).

The jury is still out. Mergers and acquisitions are forecast as likely to distort the U.S. economy in the aftermath of the 2020 novel coronavirus pandemic:

> Many companies are on the lookout for survival strategies that would avoid a ruinous liquidation of their assets. This means they may be more open than they ordinarily would be to private buyouts and mergers. But a wave of buyouts and mergers, though seemingly better than letting struggling companies die, would only intensify the economic inequality that has become this country's curse...
>
> Encouraging a wave of mergers and buyouts to help struggling businesses during the present economic crisis might yield a superficially impressive economic recovery—a rebounding stock market and big dividends for shareholders—while destroying what remains of the middle class in this country. It might seem that economic inequality could not get worse in this country, but it could. (Wu, 2020)

The only guaranteed winners in all of these instances are always the mergers and acquisition specialists, investment bankers, and lawyers themselves who put the deals together.

Tasks of the Strategic Manager

Based on the concepts and frameworks in these first four chapters, your job as strategist is to ascertain how your organization might evolve its strategy, monitor the macro-environment, assess the attractiveness of an industry, embrace (or eschew) diversification opportunities, and set about building an execution-capable organization by, among other possible action steps:

- Deciding upon the timing and extent of any moves to enter opportunity-rich sectors and/or exit opportunity-poor sectors to achieve organizational goals;
- Updating the utilization of the organization's resources and capabilities to match changing market conditions;
- Restructuring the organization's culture via new appraisal and incentive systems to implement change;
- Assembling a strong, diverse management team with complementary skills and talents; and
- Providing incentives for staff that are unable to cope with change to upgrade their skills or at worst, leave the organization.

In the next chapter, we will take up the routines that strategists employ in making decisions about how and where to compete to achieve the better normal.

End of Chapter Mini-Case: Mark Anthony Group

Armand Gilinsky

As Mark Anthony Group learned the hard way during its evolution from a Canadian wine producer to becoming a diversified alcoholic beverage marketing company, competition was not only coming from within the wine category of the beverage industry, but also from newly emerging categories such as spirit coolers and hard seltzer.

Company Evolution

In 1981, a 31-year-old wine rep named Anthony von Mandl bought a majority stake in a Kelowna, British Columbia vineyard, which evolved into a winery called Mission Hill Family Estate. Von Mandl's business rose to global prominence, winning best Chardonnay at the International Wine and Spirit Competition in 1994 and best Pinot Noir under £15 at the 2013 Decanter World Wine Awards and in 2019, the World's Best Vineyards Academy named Mission Hill to its annual top 50.

A. Gilinsky
Sonoma State University, Rohnert Park, CA, USA
e-mail: gilinsky@sonoma.edu

Fifteen years later, in 1996, the Marc Anthony Group, as the company was later named, subsequently launched what von Mandl dubbed as the world's first spirit cooler, Mike's Hard Lemonade, which more or less took the world by storm when it debuted in the U.S. three years later. Labatt Brewing Co. bought the Canadian rights to Mike's Hard in 2015 for a reported US$350 million; Mark Anthony still retained the American sales rights of Mike's Hard.

Twenty years passed until the U.S. release of White Claw, an alcoholic (hard) seltzer water beverage that quickly caught on with younger consumers. A recent Bloomberg report noted that Mark Anthony posted about US$4 billion in revenue for 2020. The White Claw brand managers have reportedly "been highly focused on market share from the jump and remains unrelenting in pricing and promotion initiatives designed to increase household penetration and get liquid to lips," according to a reporter from Mashed.

The Market for Hard Seltzer Beverages

The hard seltzer market was valued at $3.83 billion in 2019, sales of hard seltzer brands grew by 200% in 2020, and the category's future growth was estimated at 12.7% (compounded annually) to reach $10.0 billion by 2027, according to a report from Allied Market Research.

White Claw and Truly (owned by Boston Beer Company) comprised an estimated 85% of all hard seltzer sales in 2020. In summer 2021, Boston Beer announced that the Truly brand had entered the spirits category via an alliance with another alcoholic spirits producer, Beam Suntory.

While White Claw had been first-to-market and continued to lead the category, Boston Beer's Truly proved to be a formidable fast-follower. Truly's volume grew 60% in the year-to-date through June 13, 2021, compared with just a 0.3% advance for White Claw, according to a report by *Shanken Daily News* in August 2021. See Table 4.2 that shows market share information for the leading U.S. hard seltzer brands.

Competitors in the Hard Seltzer Market

Later entrants into the hard seltzer category also began to make inroads. Later entrants included Constellation Brands' Corona Seltzer, which launched in 2020 to attain an initial 7.5 million cases sold. Corona Seltzer

Table 4.2 Leading hard seltzer brands in the U.S. (millions of 2.25-gallon cases)

Brand	*Parent company*	*2019 Market share (%)*	*2020 Market share (%)*	*Percent change*[1]
White Claw	Mark Anthony Brands	41.9	95.0	126.8%
Truly	Boston Beer Co	20.0	47.7	138.6%
Bud Light Seltzer	AB InBev	–	18.2	+
Corona Seltzer	Constellation Brands	–	7.5	+
Vizzy	Molson Coors	–	3.8	+
Smirnoff Seltzer	Diageo Beer Co USA	2.5	3.7	43.5%
High Noon Sun Sips	E.&J. Distillers	0.7	3.0	300.0%

[1] Based on unrounded data
Source Shanken Daily News / Impact Databank

was formatted in 12-pack variety packs of slim cans that featured fruit flavors including mango, cherry, lime, raspberry, and passionfruit, among others. In June 2021, Constellation launched a new Corona Hard Seltzer Limonada into U.S. national distribution.

Diageo Beer Company, which had already held a strong position in the flavored malt beverage (FMB) category with its Smirnoff Ice brand, extended its brand portfolio into hard seltzers with Smirnoff Seltzer, which sold 3.8 million cases in 2020, helping to increase Smirnoff's U.S. FMB sales by 17 percent in the fiscal year ended in June 2021. The most recent offering from the brand was Smirnoff Seltzer Pink Lemonade. Earlier in 2021, Diageo announced an $80 million expansion of its U.S. ready-to-drink (RTD) capacity to produce 25 million cases of RTDs a year at its Illinois manufacturing facility.

High Noon Sun Sips, from E.&J. Distillers, reached three million cases sold in 2020, and continues to carve out space at the higher end of the category. The brand was made by combining vodka with flavors from real fruit. High Noon's control state volume more than doubled through the first half of 2021.

Brewing giants like InBev Anheuser-Busch and Molson Coors were also moving into the hard seltzer marketplace. Bud Light Seltzer launched in 2020 and reached 18.2 million cases sold. Meanwhile, Molson Coors' Vizzy brand sold 3.8 million cases in 2020, and that company also partnered with Coca-Cola to create the Topo Chico label.

New Entry Threat

Perhaps the newest entrant into the hard seltzer category was an unheralded virtual wine company based in the heart of California's central coast wine growing region, War Room Cellars. War Room drew upon the collective creative talents of nine people working out of an iconic log cabin in the hills of Santa Margarita. Forged in the wake of a group exodus of three employees from the Rabble Wine Company in 2018, War Room's original strategy was based on acquiring heritage wine brands, developing brand equity, and then selling them off for a profit to large wine companies. That strategy changed in 2020, when War Room Cellars launched its first hard seltzer brand, called Bubble Butt, in August of that year, during the COVID-19 pandemic when social distancing was required and consumers relied on online purchases and off-premise stores to purchase alcoholic beverages. As War Room did not have an online e-commerce platform, its Bubble Butt brand was initially distributed only to off-premise retailer accounts. Nine months after the launch of Bubble Butt, the company projected 2021 sales at 1,000 cases for the year and 350,000 cases in three years' time. War Room's goal was to eventually ship one million cases of Bubble Butt per annum (Millerick, 2021).

Lesson learned. Timing shapes strategy across three levels: individual, organizational, and industry. First, top management teams act in the present to secure future resources where few or none currently exist. Critical variables for success may include perseverance to learn continuously rather than always looking for quick fixes, realism of deadlines, recognition of emerging opportunities and threats, and perception of growth stage problems and matching strategy to stage of growth. Second, at the group or organizational level, scarce temporal resources must be allocated, which affects the number of strategic options pursued, the pacing of activity, and the synchronization of firm development with market readiness. At the outset, a critical choice for the Marc Anthony Group at the organizational level was to be a first mover vs. a rapid follower in the hard seltzer category.

As new rivals have entered, the Marc Anthony Group is no longer a position to reap the benefits of its previous temporary monopoly of the hard seltzer category. Third, at the industry or environmental level, timing is a factor in responses to changes in competitor power, technology shifts, product obsolescence, customer demand, and alignment of stakeholder time horizons (e.g., stakeholders including founders, investors, employees, suppliers, distributors, resellers, consumers, etc.). *Marc Anthony Group has squandered its first-mover advantage.* It can be argued that Marc Anthony Group has already waited too long for expansion, as evidenced by its flat sales growth and shrinking market share.

Management skills, organizational structure, quality control, and higher operation costs accompanying any future diversifications must be weighed with available capacity and market expansion opportunities. These issues need to be addressed by Marc Anthony Group going forward.

Further Reading

Ameer, R., & Othman, R. (2012). Sustainability practices and corporate financial performance: A study based on the top global corporations. *Journal of Business Ethics, 108*, 61–79. https://doi.org/10.1007/s10551-011-1063-y

Andrews, K. R. (1980). *The concept of corporate strategy* (2nd ed.). Richard D. Irwin.

Anon. (2020, February 5). Was Instagram the steal of the century? *The New York Times online*. Accessed February 8, 2020, from https://www.nytimes.com/2020/02/05/business/dealbook/instagram-20-billion-revenue.html

Ansoff, H. I. (1965). *Corporate strategy*. McGraw-Hill.

Bomey, N. (2020, September 9). Mall owners Simon and Brookfield to acquire J.C. Penney out of bankruptcy despite 'screaming matches.' *USA Today online*. Accessed September 13, 2020, from https://www.usatoday.com/story/money/2020/09/09/jcpenney-sale-simon-property-group-brookfield-property-partners/5761731002/.

Caddell, N. (2021, February 5). The innovators: Mark Anthony Group bottles lightning—For the second time. *BC Business Online*. Retrieved August 23, 2021 from https://www.bcbusiness.ca/The-Innovators-Mark-Anthony-Group-bottles-lightningfor-the-second-time

Cain, A., & Stone, M. (2020, August 25). These 31 retailers and restaurant companies have filed for bankruptcy or liquidation in 2020. *Business Insider.com*. https://www.businessinsider.com/retailers-filed-bankruptcy-liquidation-closing-stores-2020-2#neiman-marcus-filed-for-chapter-11-bankruptcy-on-may-7-citing-inexorable-pressure-from-the-coronavirus-pandemic-11. Accessed August 31, 2020.

Harris, M. (2020, March 6). The truth about the owner of White Claw. *Mashed Online*. Retrieved August 23, 2021 from https://www.mashed.com/192880/the-truth-about-the-owner-of-white-claw/

Isaac, M., & Griffith, E. (2020, June 30). Uber makes offer to buy Postmates delivery service. *The New York Times*. Retrieved July 5, 2020 from https://www.nytimes.com/2020/06/29/technology/uber-postmates-buy-offer.html?searchResultPosition=3

Kamble, A., & Deshmukh, R. (2020, August). Allied Market Research. *Hard Seltzer Market by ABV Content (ABV Less Than 5 percent and ABV More Than 5 percent), Packaging (Metal Cans, Glass Bottles, and Plastic Bottles), and Distribution Channel (Off-trade and On-trade): Global Opportunity Analysis and Industry Forecast 2021–2027*. https://www.alliedmarketresearch.com/hard-seltzer-market-A06785

Markides, C. (1997, November/December). To diversify, or not to diversify. *Harvard Business Review, 75*(6), 95–99.

Masheshwari, S. (2020, June 30). Lululemon to buy Mirror, fitness start-up. *The New York Times*, Section B, 3. Retrieved July 5, 2020 from https://www.nytimes.com/2020/06/29/business/lululemon-buys-mirror.html?searchResultPosition=5

Millerick, C. W. (2021, August 9). "WarRoom Cellars: Virtually Surfing the Hard Seltzer Wave." Unpublished MBA Capstone project.

Morgenson, G. (2016, September 18). Champagne for Bayer, ice water for investors. *The New York Times*, Section B, 1.

Penn, C. (2021a, February). Outlook & trends: What we can learn from 2020: WBM Top 50. *Wine Business Monthly*, pp. 12–28.

Penn, C. (2021b, February). State of the Wine Industry, 2021. *Wine Business Monthly*, pp. 16–26.

Porter, M. E. (1979, March-April). How competitive forces shape strategy. *Harvard Business Review*, pp. 137–145.

Porter, M. E. (1980). *Competitive strategy*. The Free Press.

Porter, M. E. (1985). *Competitive advantage: Creating and sustaining superior performance*. Free Press.

Porter, M. E. (2008, January). The five competitive forces that shape strategy. *Harvard Business Review*, pp. 79–93.

Sullivan, D. (2021, August 12). Competition heats up in the hard seltzer category. *Shanken News Daily online*. Retrieved August 15, 2021 from https://www.shankennewsdaily.com/index.php/2021/08/12/29222/competition-heats-up-in-the-hard-seltzer-category/#more-29222

Wu, T. (2020, July 5). Better buyouts. *The New York Times*, SR 10. Retrieved July 5, 2020 from https://www.nytimes.com/2020/06/30/opinion/sunday/mergers-buyouts-economy-inequality.html?searchResultPosition=2

CHAPTER 5

Competing

Abstract In this chapter, you will learn about how strategic orientation shapes the selection of competitive strategies.

Keywords Competitive strategies · Cooperation and coopetition · Entrepreneurs · Formal vs. planned · Niche strategies · Strategic orientation

Strategy is a Hypothesis

Organizations formulate and implement **competitive strategies** to gain market share, grow sales and profits, limit risk, and manifest other advantages over their rivals. Other advantages may include superior staff retention and morale, innovation, reputation with customers, and speed to market. Most if not all of challenges in developing a competitive strategy relate to the inextricable linkage between external market pressures such as environmental and competitive forces and organizational orientations with respect to attaining stability or growth. Refer back to Table 1.1 in Chapter 1 that illustrates several different types of competitive strategies. Competitive strategies are in general a hypothesis that will be tested in the marketplace, or "best guess" about the future status of the organization with respect to its industry rivals.

A. Gilinsky, *Business Strategy for a Better Normal*,
https://doi.org/10.1007/978-3-031-28708-4_5

The most difficult task of any organization is to narrow down the strategic choices and prioritize, using defensible assumptions and realistic metrics to support any choice(s). Good management can galvanize an organization to operate via admirable core (social) values, producing products and services to aid economic development and well-being. Core values guide what organizations put into practice. "Walking the talk" when it comes to upholding core values when formulating and acting on a competitive strategy is considered socially responsible business behavior (although many top management teams are by no means "perfect" at accomplishing this).

Some organizations use sourcing and quality control functions to rein in costs and maintain environmental responsibility. Others walk a tightrope, balancing the preservation of a high-quality brand image, hometown culture, and equity with any future geographical expansion opportunities. All organizations are striving to develop distinctive competencies (valued, rare, and otherwise) to overtake established rivals. But how do you do this to achieve a better normal, when one of the most prized distinctive competencies, employee retention, is increasingly difficult to achieve? In the words of Derek Thompson (2021):

> ...the basic terms of employment are undergoing a Great Reset. The pandemic thrust many families into a homebound lifestyle reminiscent of the 19th-century agrarian economy—but this time with screens galore and online delivery. More families today work at home, cook at home, care for kids at home, entertain themselves at home, and even school their kids at home. The writer Aaron M. Renn has called this the rise of the DIY family, and it represents a new vision of work-life balance that is still coming into focus. By eliminating the office as a physical presence in many (but not all!) families' lives, the pandemic may have downgraded work as the centerpiece of their identity...[but] business formation has surged since the beginning of the pandemic, and the largest category by far is e-commerce...[it's] a centrifugal moment in American economic history.

Strategic Orientations

Business organizations can be classified as entrepreneurial, family, or traditionally managed.

Most **entrepreneurial businesses** have a bias toward rapidly taking action to pursue opportunity and making the most of any windows of opportunity. Some refer to this as a "Ready, Fire, Aim!" approach.

Entrepreneurs are able to quickly withdraw their resources from a particular opportunity, that is, if initial feedback from the pursuit of an opportunity suggests that it might not be the right time for the company, losses from the initial pursuit may be minimized. New, entrepreneurial business formations have been driven by the presence or generation of opportunities for new entry, and the entrepreneurs starting these ventures tend to be less concerned about the resources that may be required to pursue opportunities. The presence or lack of resources does not constrain the strategic thinking of an entrepreneurially managed firm, particularly in the e-commerce space.

Family businesses are either owned and operated by family members (family-run) or owned by family members and operated by trained managers who are not family members (professionally run). Family-run businesses are characterized by the routinized organizational behaviors and shared sense of responsibility that the family feels toward the business. Family leaders typically avoid risk and seek stable growth as part of their commitment to the long-term success of the business (Eddleston & Kellermanns, 2007).

Professionally managed companies tend to place considerable emphasis on information-driven decisions derived from data collection and analysis. Doing so helps managers determine the return on resources to be deployed. In contrast to entrepreneurial and family-managed businesses, professional managers are more apt to be systems-oriented in terms of building the structure to support the future growth of the business. One might say that the entrepreneurs are the idea people in the business, and the administrators make the business work.

See Table 5.1, A typology of strategic orientations.

Using an assessment of how well the strategic elements fit, analysts can identify which gaps exist in an entrepreneurial venture and also how to fill them. "Bootstrapping" via other people's money or other people's sweat equity (often, via franchising a concept) is a typical means to bridge those gaps.

Top management teams' orientations toward strategy have been characterized by Mintzberg (1973) as either emergent or planned. Strategic intent may be directed toward satisfying existing customers' needs or seeking new customers and developing innovative products and services to meet those needs (Daily & Dollinger, 1994; Porter, 1985). Miles and Snow's (1978) typologies (Reactor, Defender, Analyzer, and Prospector) and Ireland and Hitt's (1997) approach to time-based

Table 5.1 A typology of strategic orientations

Managerial characteristics	*Time horizon*	*Selective (Domestic or international)*	*Mass (Primarily domestic)*	*Global (Primarily international)*
Entrepreneurial	Short-term Early entrant or fast-follower	Allocator	Category creator	"Amazon"
Professionally managed	Medium-term Fast- or late follower	Niche provider	Brand steward	Portfolio builder
Family-run	Long-term Late - or never-follower	Classic/ traditionalist	Cooperative	Joint venture/strategic partner

Source Created by author for this book

strategy (first mover, early follower, in step with rivals, and late follower) can be used to classify the changing strategic orientations.

The basic dimensions of choice are whether an organization is content with its current customer-market, the *status quo*, or needs to search for new customer-markets, as indicated in Fig. 5.1.

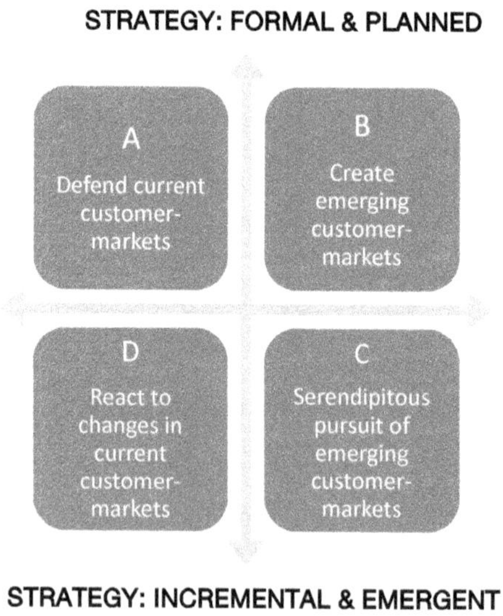

Fig. 5.1 Mapping strategic orientations (*Source* Created by author)

Quadrants

A. Need to stay in step with rivals—current market has high concentration of competitors

- Competition stable, market is characterized by few dominant, large players
- Barriers to entry often regulatory and financial
- Success sustained by raising barriers to entry or via governmental regulations deterring entry

B. Early entry is vital due to the expected high concentration of competitors

- Competition intense, aggressive
- Limited number of players due to regulatory or financial barriers
- Rapid growth opportunities for niche players to thrive

C. Must prospect for opportunistic niches or vacant segments

- Competition in chaotic market conditions and jockeying for position
- Adaptive niche strategies present greatest opportunities for success—if niches can be defended with limited resources

D. Forced to react to a saturated, fragmented market/highly competitive environment

- Companies highly vulnerable to market fluctuations and competitive forces
- Not a long-term viable segment in current customer-markets

Competitive Strategies

The basic strategy options for challengers are finding and serving niche markets; pursuing corporate social responsibility (CSR); diversifying products, services and markets served; learning from crises and trying to do something better; and venturing outside of the home market into new global markets.

Niche strategies. A gap-filling or niche strategy tends to be the preferred entry mode for most businesses. It is a common entry strategy into the market employed by new businesses, as it usually takes few resources because of lower marketing costs and the ability to start on a smaller scale. In the niche strategy, the entrepreneur finds a small part of a market that is not being served or is significantly underserved. A niche strategy typically provides a more attractive market with less competition and a more dependent set of customers. Success rates tend to be higher for niche businesses because they have less direct competition. Also, by encountering less competition, niche businesses can charge higher prices, which allows for quicker positive cash flow during start-up and better margins once profitable. However, there are a number of pitfalls to be aware of when choosing a niche strategy:

1. Entering a niche requires adaptability in the business plan. If the entrepreneur misses the mark on exactly what customers in a niche want, it doesn't matter how safe the niche is, the customers will not automatically buy.
2. Niche markets, like any market, change over time and require adaptability for success. Even though it may be considered a niche, a narrow market is not isolated and is subject to the same forces and trends that can affect all markets.
3. Niches can disappear. No market is forever. Niches are the type of market that can dry up, sometimes quite suddenly. Again, adaptation can offer entrepreneurs some hope, but if the decline is too rapid many niche businesses will fail.
4. Niches can grow—and attract unwanted rivals. While significant growth in the entrepreneur's market may not sound bad, it can attract more competitors. And if it grows large enough, it can attract much larger competitors.

Corporate Social Responsibility (CSR) and/or environmental sustainability strategies. These can provide both valuable social benefits and fulfill customer needs in a superior fashion—and lead to competitive advantage for a company. However, corporate social agendas that address only social issues may help boost a company's reputation for corporate citizenship—but are unlikely to significantly improve its competitive strength in the marketplace. The goal of a triple bottom-line measurement (profits, people, and planet) is for a company to succeed simultaneously in all three dimensions, sustainably.

Diversification strategies. As will be discussed in Chapter 6, developing new products or services, expanding geographically, or trying to capture other parts of the supply chain via producing in-house or developing sales channels are typical diversification strategies. All forms of diversification need to meet the tests of industry attractiveness, cost-of-entry, and synergy. Rarely do companies succeed at meeting all three tests. Furthermore, only in rate circumstances does diversification via acquisition pay off.

Crisis strategies. Organizations can learn from crises. Many companies will discover the need to focus on stellar quality, or more capable execution, or re-building relationships and trust with consumers. To do so, sometimes wholesale changes at the top levels of management are required to repair frayed relations with stakeholders, which can lead the organization forward into new markets or sectors, or induce rivals to develop better products and services to avoid the same mistakes.

Global strategies. Organizations can also choose to venture outside of their home markets into markets abroad, i.e., to find new suppliers or new customers. Making a global strategy successful requires patience, as managers will need to work within many national political and judicial systems to improve the infrastructure and working conditions of employees, and thereby lay the long-term foundation for generating sizable revenues and profits—once conditions are ripe for market takeoff. See Chapter 7 for coverage of global strategies and the various options that organizations can pursue to compete outside of their home markets.

Cooperation and Coopetition

Sometimes, companies choose not to "go it alone," and join forces in cooperative arrangements. Coopetition has been defined as intra-industry cooperation and collaboration in the pursuit of joint benefits (Brandenburger & Nalebuff, 1996). Contrary to the long-standing tradition in business and economics based on competition, coopetition theory posits that the simultaneous pursuit of both competition and cooperation within and between business organizations can yield higher benefits than the pursuit of competition or cooperation alone (Lado et al., 1997). The motivations for and benefits expected from coopetition strategies can be diverse (Brandenburger & Nalebuff, 1996). Synergies via coopetition strategies are beneficial when alliance partners are mutually able to increase the total value more than they could individually capture. Increasing the size of the current market or creating totally new ones is another of the most obvious motives. Firms also often wish to protect the share of the market they have been able to capture and to conquer a larger share of what remains. Sharing common interests can place companies in a good position to engage in competition against rival networks, provide for resource pooling, allow for risk-sharing, and combine forces on innovations that may otherwise be impossible for each firm (Gnyawali & Park, 2011).

By way of example, wine industries across the world are considered by some industry observers to be both highly cooperative and competitive (Crick, 2018). For example, in the Old World, most French appellations practice coopetition to a greater or lesser degree through "Unions des Producteurs," and in Spain, there is the emerging group of sparkling wine producers known as Corpinnat. These companies share promotional activities and establishing joint technical standards. The Union des Côtes de Bordeaux, coopetition was directly responsible for five small appellations combining under an "umbrella" appellation, and with both horizontal and vertical cooperation in introducing a new product to the market. In Spain, according to Ton Mata, Managing Director of Recaredo, a sparkling wine producer from the Penedés region, "There is such pressure on the area to change but we have to change within the industry of we are to protect the growers. Corpinnat is the way forward for us five producers, or, we will die from competition with Prosecco and Champagne. In 10–15 years, we hope to have 2,000 members."[1]

Nevertheless, the simultaneous pursuit of both cooperation and competition has been conceptualized as a paradox because these two strategies are contradictory and opposed to each other (Lado, et al., 1997). A growing body of literature explores the success factors needed in order to reap the benefits of coopetition. Chin et al. (2008) suggested that top management buy-in and effective communication are crucial elements for successful coopetition. More recent developments have emphasized the role of integration mechanisms in enabling successful

[1] Author's personal conversation with Ton Mata, managing director of Recaredo, in Sant' Sadurni, Spain, September 23, 2019.

coopetition. For example, Gnyawali and Park (2011) identified coopetition mindsets, coopetition experience, and resources and capabilities as key factors. Leaders need awareness of the sources of tension as well as the benefits from coopetition, and executional capabilities, or the ability to design, put in place, and leverage "inter-firm relationship" routines in effectively managing the coopetition paradox (Gnyawali et al., 2016: 14).

The ability of managers to recognize and manage tension and conflicts inherent in coopetition is a paramount factor in managing coopetition. Tension can arise at multiple levels, that is, between companies, within companies, and among individuals who run those companies. Some of the biggest sources of tension among partners in a cooperative effort are (a) the common creation yet private appropriation of value and (b) the possibility of revealing proprietary information and other trade secrets key to competitive advantage (Le Roy & Fernandez, 2015).

Regardless of which strategy is selected or added to an existing repertoire of strategies, organizations tend to place considerable emphasis on information about whether an environment is opportunity-rich or opportunity-poor. Information is derived from data collection and analysis to determine, say, the return on resources to be deployed. Why? If the traditionally managed firm chose to pursue any given opportunity, it would likely be with a much larger initial investment and the intention of remaining in that line of business for a considerable length of time.

End of Chapter Mini-Case: Coinbase

Armand Gilinsky

As a digital payment system, the advantages of cryptocurrencies are that they allow for digital global payments that are fast, secure, irreversible, pseudonymous, free of government intervention, and open to any individual that wants to participate in the system. One of the recognized flaws with cryptocurrencies is that they are not backed by tangible assets or protected by a government entity. Uses of cryptocurrencies can lose a lot of money due to theft or market collapse. Would these drawbacks be held in check with the advent of more secure and stable crypto providers such as Coinbase?

A. Gilinsky
Sonoma State University, Rohnert Park, CA, USA

Crypto Defined

The "crypto" part of the term references the idea that cryptocurrencies rely on strong cryptography that prevents a security breach. Blockchain technology is the underlying process that enables the existence of cryptocurrencies. Blockchain is a digital, decentralized ledger that allows for, and keeps a record of, peer-to-peer transactions across a network without the need for a centralized third party. Blockchain technology has the potential to create enormous gains in efficiency and tremendous cost savings by eliminating the need for a third party in transactions. Three finance researchers at the Lee Kong Chian School of Business noted that, "Cryptocurrencies can be a good option to help diversify portfolio risks because the correlations between cryptocurrencies and traditional assets are consistently low and the average daily return of most cryptocurrencies is higher than that of traditional investments" ([Lee et al., 2018: 19).

Coinbase's Founding and Evolution

At its introduction in 2009 by Satoshi Nakamoto (a pseudonym) as the first cryptocurrency trading system, Bitcoin was described as a new electronic peer-to-peer cash system with no server or central authority. In the decade following Bitcoin's debut, the leading U.S.-based cryptocurrency exchange, Coinbase positioned itself, according to the company website, as "the reliable on-ramp into the cryptocurrency space for new and experienced cryptocurrency traders alike." Coinbase was founded in July 2011 by former Airbnb engineer Brian Armstrong and was first funded by Y Combinator. In 2012, co-founder Fred Ehrsam, a former Goldman Sachs trader, joined the company, after which Coinbase launched services to buy, sell, and capitalize on Bitcoin. By 2022, Coinbase was a public company operating in over 100 countries. Its 21 products covered three primary lines of business: (1) Coinbase Wallet and USD Coin for individuals; (2) Prime Commerce and Exchange for businesses; and (3) Cloud, Connect, and WalletLink for developers.

Coinbase's Competitive Strategy

The company's reputation, regulatory compliance, and track record as a custodian allowed it to maintain transaction fees above many of its peers despite operating in a crowded field with hundreds of competing firms trying to grab market share in the rapidly growing space. Unlike traditional exchanges in the U.S., Coinbase fulfills multiple roles in the trading ecosystem by acting as an exchange, asset custodian, and broker. Coinbase continued to branch off into adjacent businesses offering cryptocurrency collateralized loans, a crypto debit card, blockchain infrastructure support, and data analytics services.

Due to its breadth of its service offerings and the connection between cryptocurrency prices and trading revenue, Coinbase's short- and long-term results were deeply tied to the health and growth of cryptocurrencies as an asset class. Cryptocurrency adoption continued to rise in 2021, but questions regarding the long-term viability of cryptocurrency, the role of speculation in current market prices, and the potential for a more hostile regulatory environment remained unanswered. Crypto transcended Bitcoin and Coinbase, though. In the words of a *New York Times* columnist, Ezra Klein,

> [Crypto is] about what will happen when we build the foundation for truly digital economies, with digital money, digital goods, and digital ownership. It's about technologies that could unlock a renaissance of creativity or an orgy of commercialization. Or both. And it's about whether we are mistaking problems of power for problems of technology, and what might happen if we fix the technologies without changing the power structures. As everyone in this debate agrees, we made a lot of mistakes with the Internet we have. How do we avoid them on the Internet we're building?

Risk and Reward Tradeoffs

Ultimately, Coinbase felt it had created a strong position for itself in the cryptocurrency space, but the value of that position would be reliant on the long-term success or failure of cryptocurrencies. Coinbase appeared to be able to carve out a strong place in the cryptocurrency exchange industry by intentionally positioning itself as a reliable and compliant place to buy and sell cryptocurrency in an industry filled with risk, weak security practices, and uneven regulatory enforcement, even by the U.S. Commodities Futures Trading Commission (CFTC). Coinbase's reliability has allowed the company to successfully charge fees higher than many of its peers while building a large pool of liquidity on its platform.

Michael Miller, an industry analyst for *Morningstar*, noted in August 2021:

> Inside of an industry where regulatory enforcement can be spotty, Coinbase has positioned itself as a safe and fully compliant exchange that can provide institutional and retail traders a reliable platform to trade on. The company is registered in the United States and its decision to become publicly listed follows this strategy. Engagement with the U.S. regulatory regime does come with costs; Coinbase avoids listing cryptocurrencies that could be classified as unregistered securities by the SEC, limiting the number of trading pairs on its platform relative to some of its competitors….Additionally, knowing your client and anti-money-laundering compliance adds costs and, given the ethos of decentralization and privacy shared by many participants in the cryptocurrency economy, strict adherence to these procedures can chase away potential users of the platform.

Coinbase remained inherently reliant on the growth and success of Bitcoin, Ethereum, and other cryptocurrencies for generating returns on its invested capital. Cryptocurrency was still very early in its life cycle and the long-term success and viability was by no means guaranteed. Speculation on future price appreciation remained a key part of the space's appeal, particularly in the less well-known "alt coins," creating further uncertainty about the long-term value and sustainability of current prices. Without more confidence in the long-term viability of cryptocurrency as an asset class there was still too much potential for Coinbase's returns on invested capital to rapidly evaporate.

Crypto Comeuppance?

Rival crypto exchange FTX's woes in fall 2022 tore through the broader cryptocurrency ecosystem and sent cryptocurrency prices tumbling. Self-dealing between FTX and its associated firm, Alameda Research, left the exchange unable to honor client withdrawal requests, leaving customer funds trapped at the exchange. While Binance, the largest cryptocurrency exchange in the world, had looked like a potential savior for the firm, that rival company pulled out of a potential deal after a short due diligence process. This made FTX's eventual failure highly likely, though well-known venture capital providers like Sequoia Capital and Softbank had been early-stage investors in FTX, the company accelerated its search for funding options.

On November 9, 2022, after \$5bn customer withdrawals in one day, FTX had \$8.8bn of liabilities but only \$0.9bn of liquid assets (10%), and the company filed for Chapter 11 bankruptcy two days later. Founder and CEO Sam Bankman-Fried stepped down. In December 2022 Bankman-Fried faced the prospect of extradition from his company's base in the Bahamas back to the U.S.

Unlike earlier failures in 2022, retail awareness and trust in FTX was significant and the company was a major advertiser in the U.S., going so far as to purchase stadium naming rights in Miami. Although founder Sam Bankman-Fried had communicated regularly with regulators and industry leaders, calls for an investigation into his practices by the Securities and Exchange Commission were growing. The severe events of fall 2022 left Coinbase unprofitable. Another failure on this scale of FTX's will likely have a chilling effect on investor interest in cryptocurrency.

Lessons learned. Bold strategies involve making difficult choices and placing bets on the future. Competing successfully is not about eliminating risks, but instead about increasing the odds of success. In sorting through the possibilities of what a company or decision-maker should and should not do, managers may conclude some opportunities are unrealistic or not sufficiently attractive to pursue. However, innovative strategy-making that results in a powerful customer value proposition or pushes the company into new markets will likely require the development of new resources and capabilities and force the company and its management team outside their comfort zone. Departing from past routines indicates a desire for unique experiences, not necessarily a desire for ownership of things. Students should be able to discuss their experiences as consumers of the sharing economy (with Airbnb, DoorDash, Drizzly, GrubHub, Uber, Lyft, and other similar companies). For example, Airbnb provides customers with opportunities to experience multiple, unique accommodations not typically associated with larger chain brands. Smaller sole proprietors such as bed and breakfasts may be accessed through the app. Those offering accommodations share in the desire to not only have a unique experience with a guest, but also to invite a stranger into their own home or apartment. Moving outside of a comfort zone, moreover, may indicate a desire to access experiences immediately through smartphone technology. Students should note that a company like Airbnb could only exist since the advent of Internet and smartphone technologies. Apps and smartphones have provided the consumer the opportunity to have immediate access, such as purchasing securities and other investments, streaming songs immediately only after hearing them on the radio, or even the simple act of "googling" and looking-up information.

Consumers—especially the Millennials, Gen-Z, and later generations (i.e., those consumers born between the early 1980s and the early years of the twenty-first century)—are less technology averse, use smartphones and apps, and are more willing to experiment and embrace the "experience economy" than previous generations, and this trend should continue to occur. As these generations that have used smartphones from childhood age and get older, technology and businesses such as Bitcoin and Coinbase will seem less unusual and become more commonplace, while rivals that pursue unsound competitive strategies, like FTX, will likely fall by the wayside.

End of Chapters Strategic Planning Exercises

Leaving My Comfort Zone

How often do you challenge yourself and leave your comfort zone in order to try new things? In general, how often do you do things that are new and challenging in some way? For example, when did you last try a new hobby, sport, or activity? Visit a new place? Make friends with people who are different than you? Taste new foods or beverages? Learn new skills? Take classes in subjects you're not good at? Or, seek out a place that is an adventure beyond the parameters of what you've experienced so far?

Create a journal entry (written) or Instagram story (video) explaining the adventure or even travel activity that pushed you out of your comfort zone and describe what the experience felt like—good and bad? Did you eventually find a comfortable niche while doing this activity?

Further Reading

Anon. (2021, October 19). Coinbase strategy teardown. *CB Insights online*, Retrieved October 22, 2021 from: https://www.cbinsights.com/research/report/coinbase-strategy-teardown/

Brandenburger, A., & Nalebuff, B. (1996). *Co-opetition*. Doubleday Press.

Chin, K. S., Chan, B. L., & Lam, P. K. (2008). Identifying and prioritizing critical success factors for coopetition strategy. *Industrial Management and Data Systems, 108*(4), 437–454.

Daily, C. M., & Dollinger, M. J. (1994). An empirical examination of ownership structure in family and professionally-managed firms. *Family Business Review, 5*(2), 117–136.

Eddleston, K. A., & Kellermanns, F. W. (2007). Destructive and productive family relationships: A stewardship theory perspective. *Journal of Business Venturing, 22*(4), 545–565.

Gnyawali, D. R., & Park, B. J. R. (2011). Co-opetition between giants: Collaboration with competitors for technological innovation. *Research Policy, 40*(5), 650–663.

Gnyawali, D. R., Madhavan, R., He, J., & Bengtsson, M. (2016). The competition–cooperation paradox in inter-firm relationships: A conceptual framework. *Industrial Marketing Management, 53*(1), 7–18.

Ireland, R. D., & Hitt, M. A. (1999). Achieving and maintaining strategic competitiveness in the 21st century: The role of strategic leadership. *The Academy of Management Executive, 13*(1), 43–57.

Jones, C. P., & Jensen, G. R. (2019). *Investments: Analysis and management, 14/e*. Wiley.

Klein, E. (2021, October 15). A crypto optimist meets a crypto skeptic [The Ezra Klein Show podcast]. *The New York Times*. Retrieved October 22, 2021 from: https://www.nytimes.com/2021/10/15/opinion/ezra-klein-podcast-katie-haun.html?searchResultPosition=1

Lado, A. A., Boyd, N. G., & Hanlon, S. C. (1997). Competition, cooperation, and the search for economic rents: A syncretic model. *Academy of Management Review, 22*(1), 110–141.

Lee, D. K.C., Guo, L., & Wang, Y. (2018). Cryptocurrency: A new investment opportunity? *Journal of Alternative Investments. 20*(3), 16–40. Research Collection Lee Kong Chian School of Business. https://ink.library.smu.edu.sg/lkcsb_research/5784

Le Roy, F., & Fernandez, A. S. (2015). Managing coopetitive tensions at the working-group level: The rise of the coopetitive project team. *British Journal of Management, 26*(4), 671–688.

Miles, R. E., & Snow, C. C. (1978). *Organizational strategy, structure, and process*. McGraw-Hill.

Miller, M. (2021, August 29). A surge in cryptocurrency prices drives a strong second quarter for Coinbase. *Morningstar Equity Analyst Report*.

Mintzberg, H. (1973). Strategy-making in three modes. *California Management Review, 16*, 44–53.

Porter, M. E. (1985). *Competitive advantage: Creating and sustaining superior performance*. Free Press.

Thompson, D. (2021, October 15). The great resignation is accelerating, *The Atlantic*. Retrieved October 17, 2021. from: https://www.theatlantic.com/ideas/archive/2021/10/great-resignation-accelerating/620382/

CHAPTER 6

Diversity, Equality, Inclusion and Diversification

Abstract In this chapter, you will learn about corporate diversification in the context of meeting social sustainability goals such as diversity, equality, and inclusion (DEI) and how those concepts relate to core values and the 3S Model discussions in Chapter 1.

Keywords Diversification · Diversity · Equality · Inclusion · Scope

Introduction

The dirty little secret of strategy is that most companies consider revenue enhancement and cost containment to be their overriding objectives. Period.

This chapter provides an overview of the way that organizations, whether they be small businesses or large corporations, can broaden their understanding of diversity so that it moves beyond legal compliance to become a major component of strategy with a distinct contribution to competitive advantage, which can be obtained from acknowledging diversity, internally and externally (Cox, 2001). Demographic changes in the workforce and customer populations, combined with global markets and international competition, result in increasingly diverse markets and workplaces.

A. Gilinsky, *Business Strategy for a Better Normal*,
https://doi.org/10.1007/978-3-031-28708-4_6

Strategists need to broaden their understanding of both these aspects of diversity and include diversity as an integrated strand within corporate strategy (David, 2009). As of April 2022, many U.S. lawmakers had proactively passed legislation promoting diversity, equity, and inclusion in the workplace (Janisch, 2022). With the exception of the state of Mississippi, as of 2022, every other U.S. state had a pay equity law on the books, which prohibited employers from discriminating against workers based on:

- Age
- Race
- Creed
- Color
- Sex
- Sexual orientation
- Gender identity
- National origin
- Religion
- Disability

The #MeToo movement also led to more far-reaching diversity, equity, and inclusion laws, which mandated harassment-prevention training, expanded protections under equal pay, and salary history bans.

But how are these objectives linked to embracing the diversity, equality, and inclusion (DEI) missions, goals, and core values illustrated in Chapter 1? Recall that an organization's core values have been very useful in setting the stage for strategy. Some key points to bear in mind:

Diversity is not an initiative but a description of "who a company is." Diversity is often imagined along two dimensions: visible and invisible traits. Visible traits include an individual's age, gender, and ethnic background. Invisible (hidden) traits include religion, sexual orientation, and socioeconomic status. However, it is essential to note that these distinctions only sometimes hold. For example, disabilities can be both visible or invisible.

Diversity can also have different meanings depending upon different cultural contexts. For example, Lori Billingsley, the chief diversity officer for the Coca-Cola Company, defines diversity from an American perspective as "the differences you can see or describe in people." This concept differs from diversity's meaning in France, where it often refers to gender diversity, or in Arab cultures, where it often refers to religious diversity (Brownlee, 2019).

Equality recognizes that each person has different circumstances and allocates resources and opportunities for all to reach an equal outcome.

In other words, equality gives everyone in the business a chance to participate…no one is excluded from that desired outcome, regardless of race, gender, religion, or other individual attributes. Equity and equality are also often assumed to be similar concepts. However, there is a significant difference between these two. The Government Alliance on Race and Equity (GARE), describes "equality and equity are sometimes used interchangeably, but actually convey significantly different ideas. Equity is about fairness, while equality is about sameness" (Nelson et al., 2015).

Equality is, therefore, concerned with treating everyone the same; whereas equity is about offering different types of support (various resources) to ensure everyone has a fair chance of success (Kranich, 2005).

Inclusion makes sure that diversity is reflected at every level of decision-making within a group. Inclusion refers to "a cultural and environmental feeling of belonging," which can be measured in the organization through the degree/extent to which employees are valued, respected, accepted, and encouraged to participate fully in the company's activities.

The National Association of Colleges and Employers defines inclusion as "authentically bringing traditionally excluded individuals and groups into processes, activities, and decision/policy making in a way that shares power and ensures equal access to opportunities and resources" (Armstrong, 2019).

All in all, trust makes it possible for companies to create an environment where everyone regardless of origin, orientation, or beliefs, feels safe to express their opinions freely and honestly. Diversity, equity, and inclusion are thus reflective of an organization's core values, as shown in Fig. 6.1.

Referring back to the list of companies in Table 1.1 in Chapter 1, Table 6.1 presents each company's DEI goals and commitments from 2021 through mid-2022.

Core values that decry racism and prejudice are fundamental to establishing DEI as an important and relevant platform for strategy-making.

Fig. 6.1 How DEI reflects an organization's core values (*Source* Brookhaven National Laboratory, Diversity, Equity and Inclusion Council https://www.bnl.gov/do/id/)

Table 6.1 Examples of Company DEI Goals and Commitments

Company	*DEI Goals*	*DEI commitments in 2021–2022*
AirBnB	By the end of 2025, it is our goal that 20 percent of U.S. employees will identify as underrepresented minorities and, at every level, 50 percent of our global employees who identify in the gender binary will be women. To help achieve these goals, we will continue to take deliberate actions to make our recruiting, promotion, and retention practices more inclusive. We continue to implement and uphold policies and programs to foster belonging in our workplace	Developed Diversity & Belonging Plan for • Established Diversity Council • Expanded training around diversity and bias removal • Required women and underrepresented minorities in the U.S. to be presented as candidates for new hires • Supported non-traditional career paths to provide people from non-traditional technical backgrounds with an entry point to an engineering career at Airbnb • Conducted annual pay equity analyses to identify and adjust potential pay gaps • Increased investment in professional development, mentorship, and sponsorship for women and underrepresented minorities, as well as those who actively advance diversity and belonging • Supported 19 employee resource groups to foster a sense of belonging at work

(continued)

Table 6.1 (continued)

Company	*DEI Goals*	*DEI commitments in 2021–2022*
Athleta (Gap)	For us, inclusion isn't optional—it's a strategic priority. Creating a culture of belonging is as critical to the success of our company as it is for the communities we serve; ultimately, a more diverse and inclusive business is a more creative, productive, and sustainable one. This report demonstrates the progress we have made toward meeting our 2025 commitments, from strengthening the pipeline of diverse talent to annually affirming equal pay across racial and gender lines. On behalf of everyone touched by our business, we are dedicated to the ongoing work required to build a more equitable industry and more just society	76 percent of global workforce are female • 42 percent of board of directors are women • 58 percent of officer positions are women • 55 percent of U.S. workforce are people of color • 40 percent of U.S. workforce are women of color • 24 percent of Technology teams are women
Chick-fil-A	One of Chick-fil-A's cornerstones is the importance of treating everyone with honor, dignity, and respect. Recently, this commitment took on special significance for us as we proactively pursued new ways to work against racism, systemic or subtle, throughout the communities we serve. Diversity, Equity, and Inclusion is directly linked to our corporate purpose, and we're building the infrastructure to incorporate this integral work into every part of our organization systemwide. Identifying opportunities to positively influence change beyond our restaurants	Announced that $5 million in True Inspiration Awards™ grants in 2020 and 2021 would be focused on Black-led nonprofits and those serving communities of color

Company	*DEI Goals*	*DEI commitments in 2021–2022*
Friedman's Home Improvement	None public yet	None public yet
GameStop	None public yet	None public yet
LinkedIn	We envision a workforce that reflects the communities we serve, and diversity, inclusion, and belonging (DIBs) remain our number one talent priority	Grew the Black leader, manager, and senior IC population by 35.0 percent, and the equivalent Latino population by 20.3 percent • placed an emphasis on gender diversity globally • Made progress in the representation of women in technical roles, which grew at 1.3 pp in 2021, representing "progress with a mix of enthusiasm for the momentum we have established and deep humility in recognizing that we have more work to do."
Lululemon	Our goal is to reach 40 percent racially diverse representation for our stores, and 30 percent racially diverse representation of our directors and assistant store managers and above by 2023. The funding and launch of a global internship and global mentorship programs will support our commitments to attract and retain more diverse talent	Provided an additional $3 million to our social impact program, Here to Be, for a total of $7 million in 2020, to disrupt inequity in well-being through movement, mindfulness, and activism • Outfitted stores with signage stating stance against racism, discrimination, harassment, and hate • Created house rules for social media channels that echo a "no-tolerance policy" of these behaviors

(continued)

Table 6.1 (continued)

Company	*DEI Goals*	*DEI commitments in 2021–2022*
Sephora	We pledged to make the Sephora experience more inclusive and equitable, for our team members, clients and the broader beauty community. To realize these commitments, we created a holistic strategy named the Sephora D&I Heart Journey, supported by 11 internal D&I task forces and a detailed Action Plan to tackle bias across all aspects of our organization	Developed a new hiring toolkit for recruiters and hiring managers to raise awareness of unconscious bias and recruit a diverse pipeline of talent • Launched the Sephora Talent Incubator program to develop the next generation of culturally competent and diverse leaders • Provided DEI mentoring and coaching for 50 managers across corporate, distribution centers, and stores
Tesla	Provide transparency in our DEI programs, identify areas of improvement, celebrate successes, and continually iterate and improve our DEI approach; Integrate accountability measures into our business operations; Focus on sustainable solutions that solve problems at the root cause and reimagine new programs with DEI principles embedded in the design; Share knowledge throughout all levels of the organization to aid in personal and professional learning and development	Created an action plan to attract, develop, and retain talent • Incorporated DEI principles into talent management (i.e., consistent and fair performance • Expanded leadership development team with a focus on providing DEI offerings to all our U.S. employees• Introduce new hires to DEI principles on their first day as part of orientation • Provided virtual instruction on unconscious bias, inclusive interviewing, and inclusive leadership

Company	*DEI Goals*	*DEI commitments in 2021–2022*
Ulta Beauty	Ulta Beauty recognizes the importance of elevating, celebrating, and consistently supporting the influence underrepresented voices bring to the beauty industry. As a values-driven company, we believe we have a responsibility to drive diversity, equity, and inclusion in our company, industry, and world. Our forward-looking DEI 2022 commitments ensure that we remain energized, creative, and extremely dedicated to leading in this critical space	Dedicated $25 million in media investments in 2022 with multicultural platforms to nurture personal connections with Latino, Black, and other multicultural beauty enthusiasts • Planned on building upon our newly established and widely proclaimed MUSE platform with programming to magnify, uplift, support, and empower Black voices in beauty • Invested $8.5 million to brand marketing support for Black-owned, Black-founded, and Black-led brands within our assortment, more than doubling last year's investment to reflect our expanded Black-owned assortment

Sources company websites and associated company DEI reports, accessed August 30, 2022

Organizations bear full responsibility for addressing stereotypes and prejudice in the workplace, particularly in cases where multiple incidents arise (Rattan & Dweck, 2018).

According to leadership scholar Richard McCline (2022):

> Wanting to achieve a common goal(s) that we have shorthanded as "success" is not enough to really guide behavior. We recognize now that we must devote upfront time on thinking through what are the beliefs that guide behavior…when no one is looking…when a "north star" is needed to avoid or at least minimize greed, selfishness, and plain old evil…when temptation blurs the line between right/wrong. Whereas culture is the internal application of the values that make up an organization, the ***culture*** of an organization…how we do things around here including our norms, rituals and Core Values…is a powerful driver of organization/group actions, regardless of how carefully thought out a Strategy may be.

Consider some recent statistics:

- Nearly six in 10 Millennials (56%) believed that CEOs have a greater obligation for speaking out about social causes than they used to (Weber Shandwick, 2017).
- Six S&P 500 and Fortune 500 companies had Black CEOs in 2021; 40 had Asian American CEOs, and Latinx/Hispanic executives led 20; as of January 2022, women held 32 (6.4%) of all CEO positions at S&P 500 companies.[1]
- Companies led by CEOs that made public commitments to DEI saw nearly 10% greater return on assets than their nonethical counterparts (Kiel, 2015).
- A company's inability to address inequities could lead it to lose ground in the war for talent; for example, 60% of all workers and 75% of workers under 40 said they wouldn't take a job, or had left a job since 2020, because the employer failed to address racism within the organization or speak out against racial injustice (Boyle, 2022).
- The COVID-19 pandemic prompted white-collar and so-called frontline workers to reassess their careers, sending quit rates to record highs. Remote work has appealed to many underrepresented

[1] See https://www.catalyst.org/research/women-ceos-of-the-sp-500/ and Kurt, D. (2022, February 28). Corporate leadership by race. Investopedia. Retrieved August 9, 2022 from: https://www.investopedia.com/corporate-leadership-by-race-5114494

minorities, according to researchers, as it could shield them from the verbal and nonverbal slights they had often faced in office environments (Boyle, 2022).

- Researchers have found a positive relationship between unrelated diversification strategies, i.e., when a firm enters an industry that lacks any important similarities with the firm's existing industry or industries, and firm corporate social performance, which raises the possibility that unrelated diversification may do greater good for society than inaction (Kang, 2015).

Why DEI?

Most companies seek compliance with laws and regulations to achieve social legitimacy. For others, DEI systems are viewed as likely to enhance a firm's performance in a variety of ways, including the areas of innovation, net profit margin, return on assets, and corporate social responsibility.

An organization's corporate social responsibility performance can increase when a diverse group of employees identifies a wider variety of ways the organization can contribute to sustainable outcomes for customers, suppliers, and communities (Ali & Konrad, 2017). Other businesses make it their clear intent to leverage their revenues and thereby maintain, if not increase their share of the market via the knowledge and talents of a diverse internal workforce, proven to contribute to creative thinking and improved capacity for innovation (Von Bergen, et al., 2005; Wheeler, 2010). These strategic orientations guided an immigrant, Cinthya Cisneros, as she founded her bakery and brewpub business, as described in the mini-case below.

Illustrative Example: La Cheve Bakery & Brews

Lisa Escalante, Caroline Evans, Julianna Flores and Talia Gamble

Cinthya Cisneros arrived in Napa, California at the age of four, immigrating from La Piedad de Cabadas in Michoacán, Mexico. She graduated from Vintage High School with an interest in chemistry. The Napa County

L. Escalante · C. Evans · J. Flores · T. Gamble
Sonoma State University, Rohnert Park, CA, USA

Hispanic Network provided Cinthya with scholarships to continue her education after high school. She earned a Bachelor of Science degree in chemistry from Sonoma State University and a single-subject teaching credential in chemistry from Sacramento State University.

In 2018, while teaching at River City High School in west Sacramento, Cinthya would often end her workday at a coffee shop that also served beer on tap, piquing Cinthya's interest in crafting beers. She subsequently took a part-time job at Stone Brewing Company in Napa and brewing classes at the University of California at Davis.

Later that year, Cinthya presented the idea to start her own brewery to her family, and invited her father to his first brewery to experience crafting different types of beers. Her father noted the family friendly environment and fell in love with the idea. Soon afterward, Cinthya, alongside her father, mother, and grandmother worked together crafting beers in the garage. In 2020 her bakery and brewpub restaurant, La Cheve Bakery & Brews, opened in the midst of the COVID-19 pandemic.

La Cheve means "the beer" in Spanish. The team operating the business comprised Juana Cisneros, Cinthya's mother, head baker; Ezquiel Cisneros, her father, cooks and repairs house equipment; Angel Aguirre, Cinthya's maternal uncle, head cook; Carlos Calderon, one of Cinthya's nephews, was also a cook. Another 22 community members made up the team. Their craft beer taproom and a restaurant offered conchas, chilaquiles, and rotating house brews. The facility was located in the oldest building in Napa, the Old Adobe House, built in 1845 by Don Cayetano Juarez.[2] The only remaining adobe and oldest structure in Napa County represented Mexican tradition.

In 2021, Cinthya was honored as a recipient of the *North Bay Business Journal's* Latino Business Leadership Award. Cinthya related her story to the *North Bay Business Journal*:

> Our strong core values encompass giving back to our community and to our employees. We opened during COVID so we've just learned to adjust quickly…COVID has shaped exactly how we operate our little home. It

[2] Juarez was granted the land by General Vallejo. Born in Monterey, California in 1807, Don Mariano Guadalupe Vallejo was a Californio general, statesman, and public figure. He was born a subject of Spain, performed his military duties as an officer of the Republic of Mexico, and shaped the transition of Alta California from a territory of Mexico to the U.S. State of California.

has taught me to continue being comfortable with being uncomfortable. You have to be ready with any challenge and acclimate as fast as you can. We can't get too comfortable anymore.

Being undocumented was extremely difficult, it challenged me in every way possible: financially, educationally, mentally. I highly value and support community programs, so now La Cheve donates proceeds to some of these local programs and has partnered with some of them to create and provide scholarships for our young community. I need to pay it forward. No question about it. I am so proud to see more and more businesses owned by Latinas, it truly warms my heart to see our culture out in our community. We all need role models, and we are definitely putting some faces out there for our younger generation to come…and that is just so exciting.

I joined Napa County Hispanic Network and donated to give high school students college scholarships. It is amazing to be able to do this for an organization that helped me. We supported a member of Napa's at-risk youth by providing a scholarship for an undocumented student through If Given a Chance, a Napa nonprofit that helps local high school students continue their education. This scholarship, called 'American Dream,' will go to a Dreamer student, said Cisneros, referring to a student protected by Deferred Action for Childhood Arrivals, or DACA, federal policy. Cisneros has also partnered with If Given a Chance on events.

Cinthya aspired to pass her bakery down to future generations while continuing to promote and educate customers about Mexican culture. In the meantime, she acknowledged that La Cheve still had work to do to find ways to enhance its competitive advantage in the local market and most importantly, pursue opportunities to diversify the business both internally and externally.

Linkages with Diversification Strategies

Revenue enhancement. As we saw in Chapter 5, many companies opt to grow sales revenues by widening their **horizontal scope**, otherwise known as **product/market diversification**.

Companies must anticipate that their customer bases will hold them accountable if they do not aspire to DEI goals and adopt practices that transparently move them toward those goals (Dukach, 2022a, 2022b).

Cost containment. Similarly, many companies seek ways to optimize their business models by reducing costs, thereby growing their profits and

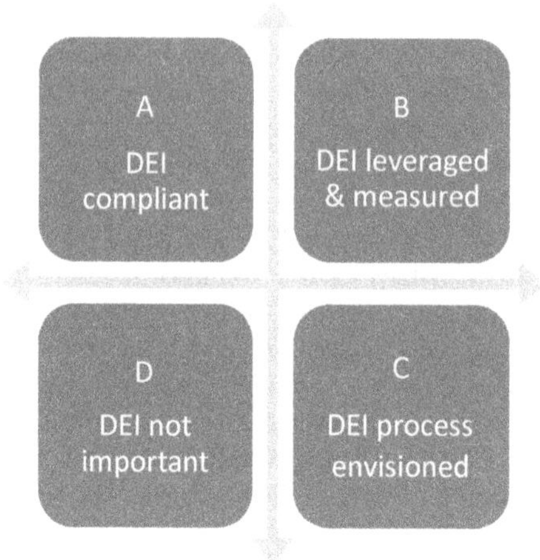

Fig. 6.2 DEI and diversification (*Source* Created by author for this book)

returns on investment. This strategy is also known as increasing a company's vertical scope. Doing so often involves integration, that is, either rearward, for example, taking over the production of raw materials for use in manufacturing products, or forward, for example into capturing supply chains for distribution and, in some cases, for direct sales. An ability to attract, retain, and motivate people from diverse cultural backgrounds, may lead to competitive advantages in cost structures and through maintaining the highest quality human resources across all stages of a business's value chain (Cox & Blake, 1991: 54).

The potential linkage between DEI and diversification strategies is shown in Fig. 6.2.

Quadrants

A. **A.**DEI strategy formulation responsive to stakeholder activism and compliance (pragmatic)

- Manage DEI to minimize reputation-damaging incidents and boost image
- We want to "get this right" before making it part of any diversification effort
- We need to develop ways to measure and report on our DEI initiatives

- Company examples (from Table 6.1): AirBnB, Lululemon, Tesla Motors

B. **B.**DEI strategy leveraged for competitive advantage (knowledge-based)

- Increases innovation and profitable growth
- Central to our strategies to increase horizontal and/or vertical scope
- We are already reporting and sharing progress with stakeholders
- Company examples (from Table 6.1): Athleta (Gap), Sephora, Ulta Beauty

C. DEI strategy is desirable but no plan yet in place (commitment without resources)

- DEI is part of our vision/mission, but we have not yet implemented
- We are not yet capable of increasing our company's horizontal or vertical scope
- We are still unsure how to measure and report progress
- Company examples (from Table 6.1): Chick-fil-A, LinkedIn

D. DEI is low on the list of priorities for our company (indifferent)

- We may not see the value of DEI for our company at this time
- Diversification is not in our strategic repertoire
- Stakeholders have not requested any measures or reports
- Company example (from Table 6.1): Friedman's Home Improvement, GameStop

In the words of Carol Fulp, "having endured disruption after disruption in the marketplace, twenty-first century companies recognize the need for more innovation inside their organizations. It's essential for their survival" (Fulp, 2018: 127).

Cultural diversity in work groups can enable companies to gain a competitive advantage in creativity, problem solving, and flexible adaptation to change (Ali & Konrad, 2017). The intent is to build an ecosystem that will thrive in an inclusive economy, starting with a supply chain of companies that embrace DEI (Phillips, 2022). See Table 6.2, "Connecting DEI with Strategy," which shows the interrelationships between a company's business-level objectives and its DEI objectives.

Inequities persist. Still, some companies believe that they are embracing diversity when in fact they have only taken baby steps, that is, they have made compliance-oriented efforts to create diversity measures and introduced management processes to monitor their efforts without taking the final steps toward valuing and ultimately leveraging diversity for competitive advantage (David, 2009). Companies like Walmart, Bank of America, and Wells Fargo Bank made headline-grabbing pledges and multimillion dollar investments to address racial inequities in the wake of the death of George Floyd, a 46-year-old black man in police custody, who was murdered by a 44-year-old Minneapolis police officer, Derek Chauvin on May 5, 2020, and the ensuing protests across the country and the world, showing that inequities persist (Boyle, 2022). Take two recent examples of companies that pursued DEI strategies, Traditional Medicinals, a herbal medicines company, and Wells Fargo Bank, respectively:

> One CEO, Blair Kellison, who [until March 2022] headed up the organic tea company Traditional Medicinals, assigned Ijeoma Oluo's *So You Want to Talk About Race* as required reading for his entire management team. [Kellison] bought a copy of the book for every employee and then invited author Oluo to speak at a Zoom town hall for the entire company. The straightforward message in Oluo's book served as a kind of leveling tool for conversations. It gave everyone a common set of talking points, ideas, and even language for talking about some important actions in the way they hire and promote people. (White, 2022: 76–77)
>
> Joe Bruno, a former executive in the wealth management division of Wells Fargo, had long been troubled by the way his unit handled certain job interviews. For many open positions, employees would interview a "diverse" candidate—the bank's term for a woman or person of color—in keeping with the bank's yearslong informal policy. But Mr. Bruno noticed that often, the so-called diverse candidate would be interviewed for a job that had already been promised to someone else. He complained to his bosses. They dismissed his claims. Last August [2021], Mr. Bruno, 58, was fired. Mr. Bruno is one of seven current and former Wells Fargo employees who said that they were instructed by their direct bosses or

Table 6.2 Connecting DEI with strategy

Business-level objectives	*DEI Objectives*	*Strategic focus*	*Measurement*	*Opportunities*	*Pitfalls*
Revenue Enhancement	Accountability with customer base	Increase horizontal scope—via product/market diversification Leverage market share via the knowledge and talents of a diverse internal workforce Implement social sustainability	• Customer acquisition • Market share • Market growth rates • Rate of product innovations • Rate of new product development • Time to market • Effective market expansion • Customer attrition rates	• Linking diversity to market needs • Inclusion of diverse perspectives • Performing team-building interventions • Recruiting diverse teams • Implementing zero tolerance policies • Diversity education/ conflict management • Including diversity goals and measures in planning • Communicating success	• No or low target customer-market representation on team, missing critical perspectives • Isms—sexism, racism, etc • Phobias, e.g., Xenophobia, Gynophobia, Homophobia • Exclusion • Cultural conflict • Lack of buy-in from top management team

(continued)

Table 6.2 (continued)

Business-level objectives	*DEI Objectives*	*Strategic focus*	*Measurement*	*Opportunities*	*Pitfalls*
Cost Containment	Build ecosystem and supply chain of companies that embrace DEI	Increase vertical scope—via value chain integration (backward or forward) Create culture of inclusion and equality Assure compliance and management accountability	• Supply chain efficiencies • Cost reductions • Workforce productivity • Rate of process innovations • Effective teams • Avoided costs • Time management • Coordination across different cultures	• Linking diversity to innovation, product development • Inclusion of diverse perspectives • Implementing diversity education/awareness/ conflict management • Including diversity performance reviews in business planning • Communicating and sharing success stories	• Unidentified diversity goals • Need to examine corporate culture through a DEI lens • Lost opportunities for advancement & recognition • Low morale, low productivity • Inadequate cultural competence

Sources Created by author from research conducted by David, A. H. "Diversity, Innovation, and Corporate Strategy," in Moss, G. (Ed.). (2009). ***Profiting from diversity: The business advantages and the obstacles to achieving diversity***. Palgrave Macmillan UK; Palich. L. E. & Gomez-Mejia, L. R. (1999). A theory of global strategy and firm efficiencies: considering the effects of cultural diversity. ***Journal of Management***, *25*(4) (July), 587–607; Wheeler, M. L. (2010). Diversity as business strategy. ***Profiles in Diversity Journal***, *12*(1), 22; and White, J. D. (2022). ***Anti-racist Leadership***. Boston: Harvard Business Review Press

> human resources managers in the bank's wealth management unit to interview "diverse" candidates—even though the decision had already been made to give the job to another candidate. Five others said they were aware of the practice, or helped to arrange it. The interviews, they said, seemed to be more about helping Wells Fargo record its diversity efforts on paper—partly in anticipation of possible regulatory audits—rather than hiring more women or people of color. All but three spoke on the condition of anonymity because they were afraid of losing their jobs at Wells Fargo or their new employers. (Flitter, 2022)

Which organization would *you* choose to work for?

End of Chapter Mini-Case: DEI at Nike, Inc.

Grace Burroughs

"Nike has allocated significant capital into building its reputation as a leader on social justice issues," reported As You Sow's Workplace Equity Program Manager Meredith Benton in August 2022. "Investors have been seeking reassurance that its own practices are sufficiently implemented to protect its very valuable brand." Activist investors also requested that Nike release its company retention rate data, but no agreement for the information to be made public had been reached with Nike as of late summer 2022.

Mounting Criticism and Departures

Criticism surrounding Nike's diversity efforts had begun as early as 2019, when Alysia Montano, a six-time U.S. Track Olympian, publicly shared her story through the *New York Times*, of that she had been dropped by Nike when she revealed he was pregnant.

In 2019, Nike re-positioned some of its brand promotions to profile controversial social justice figures, such as Colin Kaepernick. Kaepernick's "Dream Crazy" ad for Nike won an Emmy in 2019.

In December 2019, about 400 Nike employees walked out to protest the brand's alleged mistreatment of women—namely runner Mary Cain,

G. Burroughs
Sonoma State University, Rohnert Park, CA, USA

who had spoken publicly a month prior about damaging experiences with Nike staff. University of Texas, Austin media scholars Jennifer McClearen and Lily Kunda, observed the discrepancy between Nike's employee experience and its justice-oriented branding, linking it to the theory of "commodity activism."

Soon thereafter, Simone Biles discontinued her sponsorship with Nike just three months before the Tokyo Olympic games in 2020. She switched to Athleta, and commented that Athleta, "was more in line with her values of supporting women and girls."

In June 2020 Nike made a $140 million Black Community Commitment, supported by investments from Michael Jordan and Jordan Brand. Nike's Black Community Commitment was directed toward organizations dedicated to social justice, education innovation, and economic opportunity for Black people.

Professional basketball player Breanna Stewart dropped her contract in 2021 with Nike after five years and picked up a new contract with Puma that allowed her to create her own shoe line.

For International Women's Day 2021, Nike promoted a short film, *We Play Real,* featuring Black women.

In May 2022, Allyson Felix, also a famous Olympics runner, came forward in an op-ed piece in the *New York Times* with her story of being let go by Nike after announcing her pregnancy. Similar to Brianna Stewart, Allyson Felix subsequently launched her own shoe and apparel line, called Saysh, which explicitly promoted women and motherhood.

Nike's Response

Nike's 2021 *Impact Report* revealed that it had increased the number of racial and ethnic minorities in the U.S. at the director level and above in the most recent year by 4.1 percentage points to 30.3%. Nike increased its representation of women globally throughout the company to 50.4%, and since 2020, increased the number of women at the director level and above globally by 3.7 percentage points to 43%. Nike prioritized the well-being of its employees by offering expanded mental health support, free counseling, financial coaching, and greater access to the company's Crisis Text Line.

In an interview with Peter Vetter, a reporter for *Footwear News* in March 2022, Nike Inc.'s former Chief Talent, Diversity, and Culture officer Felicia Mayo said,

> The last 50 years has been quite a journey in terms of what we now know as diversity, equity and inclusion. Fifty years ago we started to see early interest in DEI, but it was mainly understood through the lens of civil rights, equal protection under the law, as well as addressing voting and housing rights. Through the lens of sport, we saw moments like the 1968 Summer Olympics where athletes showed their solidarity with the civil rights movement during the medal ceremony and many other public moments. We saw shifts in society recognizing the importance of equality.

Mayo added that DEI will continue to be an all-hands-on-deck effort at Nike:

> As we celebrate our 50th anniversary, we can look back and say that we have always been a brand rooted in purpose and committed to creating an equal playing field for all. As we look to the next 50 years, we will continue on our journey, because there is no finish line.

In February 2022, Nike revealed multiple new grant recipients: Son of a Saint, All Star Code, Big Brothers/Big Sisters of America, and the Equal Justice Initiative. Nike's local investments in 2022 were anticipated to total $2.75 million and reach 44 organizations throughout the U.S., in New York City, Los Angeles, Chicago, Portland, Ore., Memphis, St. Louis, and Boston.

Nike, in partnership with the University of Southern California, also piloted a diversity and inclusion curriculum that covered anti-racism, racial inequity, and micro-aggressions to be rolled out to the entire company in late 2022. "At Nike, diversity, equity and inclusion is part of everyone's responsibility. Our entire workforce is engaged, because it will take all of us to address these societal issues and to help us advance towards our 2025 targets," Mayo said. "We have an expectation of our leadership team to focus on DEI integrated into business and have made it a part of their success metrics at the company."

The U.S. market for women's apparel. The U.S. market for women's shoes and clothing, an estimated $134 billion in 2021, exceeded that of the men's market, at an estimated $82.2 billion. Nike's sales to female shoppers represented less than 25% of the company's total revenues in fiscal 2021.

DEI Targets

Nike set targets for 2025 focused on achieving 50% representation of women in its global corporate workforce and 45% in leadership positions; 35% representation of racial and ethnic minorities in its U.S. corporate workforce; and to maintain 100% pay equity across all employee levels on an annual basis.

According to Mayo, additional targets for 2025 will be a continuation of Nike's commitment to creating a more diverse and inclusive team. These include investing in Historically Black Colleges and Universities and Hispanic-serving Institutions, equitable and competitive pay and benefits, education and professional development, and more. Also, Mayo said that Nike will focus on community commitments and partnerships, innovative career development programs, authentic and inclusive leadership curriculum, mentorship programs, and more.

Stakeholder Activism

As You Sow, a non-profit advocacy group, organized and submitted a resolution at Nike's October 2021 annual general meeting. The resolution demanded that worker recruitment and promotion data be made public and parsed out by gender, race, and ethnicity. As You Sow was also interested in learning about the efficacy of Nike's diversity and inclusion programs.

On November 29, 2021, professors at the UC Berkeley Extension Program interviewed Jarvis Sam, vice president, global diversity and inclusion at Nike Inc. During that interview, Mr. Sam stated, "Diversity fatigue comes from the idea that we're trying to handle so much at one particular time, and we're not actually taking a piecemeal approach to saying what is actually important to drive community engagement and solidarity at this time and then elevating and moving past that." The entire November 29, 2021 interview can be viewed at: https://www.youtube.com/watch?v=BwE5U7JO6wM [Time: 1:44:14].

Nike announced in August 2022 that the company was set to release selected data from its diversity and inclusion programs by the end of 2024.

Lessons learned. Companies that take actions to build a workforce that is diverse with respect to gender, race, and national origin can strive to make their workplaces attractive to all groups and perspectives. In companies where everybody feels a sense of belonging, there is likely to be a beneficial impact on the mental health of the workforce and financial health of the company (Gamble et al., 2024; Jacob et al., 2020). Millennial and Gen-Z cohorts increasingly dominate global workplaces and consumer marketplaces. These generations' concerns for social justice are continually evolving and businesses are increasingly under a microscope to determine their commitments to DEI and conclusively prove that these commitments are indeed impactful rather than merely cosmetic (Phillips, 2014; White, 2022). It is possible that well-known companies like Nike believe that they are embracing diversity when in fact the company has only yet taken a partial journey (Aureli et al., 2020).

End of Chapters Strategic Planning Exercises

DEI Awareness

Choose a company where you are currently working or are considering for a career, or for a potential investment. Do some research on the company and apply the following rubric. Sources can include company websites, LinkedIn, an investment analyst's report, or profiles in the news. What did you learn about this company?

Company	*Yes/No*	*Guiding questions*
"What"		Is DEI specified in the company's values, expectations, and mission? Has the company's customer base held it accountable for instilling DEI practices?
CEO/Board/Top Management Team	**Yes/No**	**Guiding questions**
"Who"		Is company's top management team representative of DEI? Is there evidence of respect for different perspectives among members of those groups?
Strategy	**Yes/No**	**Guiding questions**
"How"		Is there a clear relationship between DEI and financial performance? Is there a clear relationship between DEI and the company's "innovation intensity" (the ratio of research and development expenses to assets)?

Further Reading

Ali, M., & Konrad, A. M. (2017). Antecedents and consequences of diversity and equality management systems: The importance of gender diversity in the TMT and lower to middle management. *European Management Journal, 35*(4), 440–453.

Anon., (2021, October 26). Napa's La Cheve Bakery and Brews owner wins Latino business leadership award. *North Bay Business Journal* (online). Retrieved October 11, 2022 from: https://www.northbaybusinessjournal.com/article/article/napas-la-cheve-bakery-and-brews-owner-wins-latino-business-leadership-awar/

Aureli, S., Gigli, S., Medei, R., & Supino, E. (2020). The value relevance of environmental, social, and governance disclosure: Evidence from Dow Jones Sustainability World Index listed companies. *Corporate Social Responsibility & Environmental Management, 27*(1), 43–52. https://doi-org.sonoma.idm.oclc.org/10.1002/csr.1772

Armstrong, K. (2019). *What exactly is diversity, equity, and inclusion? (blog).* Retrieved December 22, 2022 from: https://community.naceweb.org/blogs/karen-armstrong1/2019/06/25/what-exactly-is-diversity-equity-and-inclusion

Boyle, M. (2022, June 9). "It's window dressing": Firms battle a trust gap on racism efforts. *Bloomberg.Com, 27*.

Colvin, C. (2022, August 4). Nike to release DEI pay data following board pressure. *HR Dive* (online). Retrieved August 6, 2022 from: https://www.hrdive.com/news/nike-dei-recruitment-promotion-data-aug-2022/628731/

Cox, T., Jr. (2001). *Creating the multicultural organization: A strategy for capturing the power of diversity* (p. 77). Jossey-Bass.

Cox, T. H., Jr., & Blake, S. (1991). Managing cultural diversity: Implications for organizational competitiveness. *Acad Mgt Executive, 5*(3), 45–56.

David, A. H. "Diversity, Innovation, and Corporate Strategy," In G. Moss. (Ed.). (2009). *Profiting from diversity: The business advantages and the obstacles to achieving diversity*. Palgrave Macmillan.

Dukach, D. (2022a) "DEI gets real," *Harvard Business Review*, *100*(1) January–February, 150–151.

Dukach, D. (2022b, March 29). Research roundup: How women experience the workplace today. *Harvard Business Review Digital Articles*, 1–6.

Flitter, E. (2022, May 20) Bank's effort on diversity just on paper. *The New York Times*, Section B, 1. Retrieved June 3, 2022, from: https://www.nytimes.com/2022/05/19/business/wells-fargo-fake-interviews.html?searchResultPosition=1

Fulp, C. (2018). *Success through diversity: Why the most inclusive companies will win*. Beacon Press.

Grant, R. M., Jammine, A. P., & Thomas, H. (1988). Diversity, diversification and profitability among British manufacturing companies, 1972–1984. *Academy of Management Journal, 31*(4), 772–801.

Hunt, V., Yee, L., Prince, S. & Dixon-File, S. (2018). "Delivering through diversity," McKinsey & Company, (www.mckinsey.com), January, 8.

Ingram, P. (2021). The forgotten dimension of diversity. *Harvard Business Review, 99*(1), January–February, 58–67.

Jacob, K., Unerman, S., & Edwards, M. (2020). *Belonging: The key to transforming and maintaining diversity, Inclusion, and equality at work.* Bloomsbury.

Janisch, K. (2022, April 13). The state of diversity, equity, and inclusion laws today. *Gov Docs*. Retrieved August 30, 2022 from: https://www.govdocs.com/the-state-of-diversity-equity-and-inclusion-laws-today/

Kang, J. (2013). The relationship between diversification and corporate social performance. *Strategic Management Journal, 34*, 94–109.

Kiel, F. (2015) Measuring the return on character, *Harvard Business Review, 93*(4), April, 20–21.

Kranich, N. (2005). *Equality and equity of access: what's the difference? American Library Association online*. Retrieved December 22, 2022 from: http://www.ala.org/advocacy/intfreedom/equalityequity

McCline, R. L. (2022). A note to the board: Conversation of core values as addendum to Deauville's vision and mission statements. Private correspondence with author, August 26, 2022.

Nelson, J., Spokane L., Ross L. & Deng, N. (2015). Advancing racial equity and transforming government. *Government alliance on race & equity: Issue lab.* Retrieved December 22, 2022 from: https://search.issuelab.org/resource/advancing-racial-equity-and-transforming-government-a-resource-guide-to-put-ideas-into-action.html

Palich, L. E., & Gomez-Mejia, L. R. (1999). A theory of global strategy and firm efficiencies: Considering the effects of cultural diversity. *Journal of Management, 25*(4), 587–607.

Phillips, K. W. (2014). *How Diversity Works. Scientific American, 311*(4), 43–47.

Rattan, A., & Dweck, C. S. (2018). What happens after prejudice is confronted in the workplace? How mindsets affect minorities' and women's outlook on future social relations. *Journal of Applied Psychology, 103*(6), 676–687.

Smith, G., McElhaney, K., & Chavez-Varela, D. (2021). The state of diversity, equity, and inclusion in business case studies. *Journal of Business Diversity, 21*(3), 63–83.

The Conference Board (2022, June 30). *Survey: Professional development is key to retaining talent, but people of color report less access*. Accessed July 25, 2022 from: https://www.conference-board.org/press/professional-development-survey-retaining-talent.

Verry, P. (2022, March 22). How Nike is progressing with its diversity, equity and inclusion commitments + its goals for 2025. *Footwear News (Online)*. Los Angeles. Retrieved August 4, 2022, from: https://footwearnews.com/2022/business/athletic-outdoor/nike-diversity-equity-inclusion-2021-impact-report-1203262446/

Von Bergen, C. W., Soper, B., & Parnell, J. A. (2005). Workforce diversity and organizational performance. *Equal Opportunities International, 24*(3), 1–16.

Weber Shandwick, (2017, July 24). *CEO activism in 2017: High noon in the C-suite*. Retrieved August 8, 2022 from: https://www.webershandwick.com/news/ceo-activism-in-2017-high-noon-in-the-c-suite/

Wheeler. (1998). Measuring diversity: A strategy for organizational effectiveness. *Employment Relations Today, 25*(1), 61–68. https://doi.org/10.1002/ert.3910250107

Wheeler, M. L. (2010). Diversity as business strategy. *Profiles in Diversity Journal, 12*(1), 22.

White, J. D. (2022). *Anti-racist Leadership*. Harvard Business Review Press.

Zimmer, J. (2021, February 9), Napa Latino family making it happen at new restaurant La Cheve, started during pandemic, *North Bay Business Journal (online)*. Retrieved October 11, 2022 from: https://www.northbaybusinessjournal.com/article/article/napa-latino-family-making-it-happen-at-new-restaurant-la-cheve-started-dur/

CHAPTER 7

Contemplating Globalization

Abstract In this chapter, you will learn that businesses have choices as well as tradeoffs in competing globally and locally.

Keywords Cross-border strategies · De-globalization · Franchising · Globalization · Multi-domestic · Transnational

Why Expand Geographically?

Supposing you have started a streetwear fashion company, let's call it "Urban Style," and wish to source production and/or seek customers outside your local or domestic market. You might choose to do so for any of five major reasons:

1. To gain access to new customers;
2. To achieve lower costs through economies of scale, experience, and increased purchasing power;
3. To gain access to low-cost inputs of production;
4. To further exploit its core competencies; and
5. To gain access to resources and capabilities located in foreign markets.

A. Gilinsky, *Business Strategy for a Better Normal*,
https://doi.org/10.1007/978-3-031-28708-4_7

So, if Urban Style is interested in pursuing global strategies, you will need to be adaptable, and patient. You will need to work within many national political and judicial systems to improve the infrastructure and working conditions of your employees, and thereby lay the long-term foundation for generating sizable revenues and profits—that is, once conditions are ripe for market takeoff.

Adapting to Global Markets

If you are considering international expansion, you may need to adapt Urban Style's business model to local conditions in other countries. There are often cross-country differences in demographics, cultural attitudes and values, and access to markets. There may often be competitive pressures to enter as a lowest cost provider or at least as a best-cost provider. You will need to study the particular characteristics of local suppliers if you are planning on manufacturing offshore, as you may need to adapt Urban Style's core values to accommodate local cultural norms.

Ethical relativism. Companies need to accept that building a local market for a company's products is most likely to be a long-term process. If the company has sufficient clout, it can try (but not always succeed) to change a local market to better match the way the company does business elsewhere. Otherwise, a company must accept the principles of ethical relativism.

Ethical relativism, according to Carroll (2004), implies that whether certain actions or behaviors are ethically right or wrong depends on the ethical norms of the country or culture in which they take place. That is, when there are cross-country or cross-cultural differences in ethical standards, it is appropriate for local ethical standards to take precedence over what the ethical standards may be in a company's home market.

> One of the most important dimensions of ethical behavior is ethical relativism, which contrasts with the notion of universal morality and focuses instead on "flexible conceptions of right and wrong based on context". (Valentine & Bateman, 2011: 157)

Managers should note that individuals working in boundary spanning roles in a cross-cultural environment are exposed to increased opportunities for unethical behavior (Melanie et al., 2020). managers may be able to reduce opportunistic behavior by implementing tactics to influence individuals' ethical perspectives to be less relativistic (Wang & Calvano, 2015), training moral competence (Gentile, 2016), and evaluating their ethical perspective when making assignment decisions. Considering ethical relativism scores as part of the assignment process may reduce unethical behavior in the presence of asymmetric information between the employee and organization. Managers may be able to maximize the benefits of cross-cultural training *if* it is coupled with ethical training to minimize the influence of an individual's ethical relativism. This will enable firms to optimally benefit from the employee's cross-cultural skills.

For example, many integrated oil companies that are headquartered in the U.S. or the European Union, countries where women are considered to have equal rights and bribery is illegal, also have operations in the Middle East, where women are considered subordinate citizens and bribery (or *baksheesh*) is considered part of doing business.

On occasion, a multinational company can develop a code of ethics that it applies more or less evenly across its worldwide operations i.e., to avoid the slippery slope that comes from having different ethical standards for different company personnel depending on where in the world they are working. A multinational company's need to contour its ethical standards to fit local customs, local notions of fair and proper individual treatment, and local business practices can sometimes give rise to multiple sets of ethical standards.

For example, Google's code of conduct is one of the ways that company puts its values into practice. According to Google's website,

> We promote the recognition that everything people do in connection with our work at Google will be, and should be, measured against the highest possible standards of ethical business conduct. Our stated commitment to the highest standards helps the company hire great people, build great products, and attract loyal users. Respect for our users, for the opportunity, and for each other are foundational to our success, and is something we need to support every day.

Can Companies Succeed Globally?

According to Hill and Jones (2004), if Urban Style is contemplating globalization, your management team must make decisions regarding:

- The need to balance the cost with the multi-brand and multi-positioning (differentiation) sides of its business model;

- The need to be responsive to local market vs. global market characteristics;
- Which overseas markets to enter;
- When to enter those markets; and
- What scale to enter those markets.

Companies seeking entry into global markets should weigh the advantages and disadvantages of various strategies (international, multi-domestic, global, and transnational) for competing globally as shown in Table 7.1. The appropriateness of those strategies will vary owing to the extent of pressures for cost reductions and local responsiveness, according to Bartlett and Ghoshal (1989)

Table 7.1 Pros and Cons of global market entry strategies

Strategy	*Advantages*	*Disadvantages*
International	• Transfer of distinctive competencies to foreign markets	• Lack of local responsiveness • Inability to realize location economies • Failure to exploit experience-curve effects
Multi-domestic	• Ability to customize product offerings and marketing in accordance with local responsiveness	• Inability to realize location economies • Failure to exploit experience-curve effects • Failure to transfer distinctive competencies to foreign markets
Global	• Ability to exploit experience-curve effects • Ability to realize location economies	• Lack of local responsiveness
Transnational	• Ability to exploit experience-curve effects and location economies • Ability to customize product offerings and marketing in accordance with local responsiveness • Ability to reap benefits of local learning	• Difficulties in implementation because of organizational problems

Source adapted by author from Bartlett, C. A. & Ghoshal, S. (1989). *Managing across borders: The transnational solution*. Boston: Harvard Business School Press

International strategies. These can involve the development of new Urban Style products and promotional efforts in its home market, then transferring those technologies and marketing expertise to other countries, while providing tight control from your company's headquarters. Porsche, a German automotive company based near Stuttgart, prioritizes central localized operations while distributing its high-performance vehicles worldwide.

Multi-domestic (or Multinational) strategies. Pursuing joint ventures with (or outright acquisition of) strong national companies and brands that are, in keeping with Urban Style's core values, sensitive to local needs and opportunities in different regions, while providing autonomous control and minimum direction from headquarters. Nestlé is often cited as a good example of a multi-domestic company that uses a unique marketing sales approach for each country or region that it enters.

Global strategies. These involve treating the world as a largely undifferentiated market by exploiting the economies associated with standardized product or service design, centralized global-scale manufacturing, while providing a strategy largely formulated and tightly controlled by Urban Style headquarters. As of this writing, Apple is most likely considered the most important global brand, selling standardized products through over 500 stores in 25 countries.

Transnational strategies. Responding simultaneously to complex, diverse, and often conflicting strategic needs, by striving for three goals—global efficiency, national flexibility and responsiveness, and diffusion of innovation. Transnational companies employ the same basic competitive approach in all countries where they operate, sell standardized products globally, strive to build global brands, and coordinate actions worldwide with strong headquarters control. This represents a think-global, act-global approach. Yet changing Urban Style's business model to build an organization capable of supporting a transnational strategy is a complex and challenging task: implementation problems associated with creating the requisite organizational structure and control systems are well documented. Large fast-food companies such as McDonald's and KFC are often cited as examples of companies that pursue transnational strategies using products developed in the U.S. and at the same time modifying their menus to cater to local tastes and preferences in different nations.

International and global strategies tend to be least appropriate in markets where local responsiveness to consumer tastes is important (e.g., in consumer food and beverage products industries, with the possible exception of sodas, beer, and spirits). At the same time, in some industries, and the fashion industry is surely an example, competitive conditions are so intense that to survive, companies must essentially do all they can to respond to pressures for cost reductions and local responsiveness.

Cross-Border Activities

Cross-border activities, such as locating manufacturing in different countries or entering into strategic alliances, could help Urban Style respond to the pressures for cost reductions and local responsiveness.

Locating activities. Differences in wage rates, worker productivity, energy costs, and the like create sizable variations in manufacturing costs from country to country. By locating plants in certain countries, firms in some industries can reap major manufacturing cost advantages because of input quality and availability, lower input costs (especially labor), relaxed government regulations, the proximity of suppliers and technologically related industries, or unique natural resources.

For example, the European aircraft consortium Airbus' research unit and sophisticated production facility in Huntsville, Alabama was deliberately situated there because of access to a pool of technically trained personnel in the US aerospace industry. A customer service center or sales office was also opened in Alabama to help cultivate strong relationships with pivotal customers such as Delta Airlines, which is headquartered in nearby Georgia.

Alternative to Urban Style making a direct investment into a foreign country, pursuit of alliances and partnerships can also create value through resource sharing and risk spreading.

Partnerships and alliances. Collaboration with foreign companies can be a favorable and potentially fruitful means for Urban Style to enter a foreign market or strengthening its competitiveness in world markets. That is, agreements with a partner could help Urban Style to:

1. Strengthen a company's ability to gain a foothold in a desirable market;
2. Capture economies of scale in production and/or marketing;
3. Fill gaps in technical expertise and/or knowledge of local markets (buying habits and product preferences of consumers, local customs, and so on);

4. Share distribution facilities and dealer networks to mutually strengthen access to buyers;
5. Refocus energies away from competition between allies and instead toward teaming up to close the gap on leading companies; and
6. Allow each partner to preserve its independence and avoid using perhaps scarce financial resources to fund acquisitions.

An example of a successful alliance formed to enter foreign markets, or strengthen a firm's competitiveness in international markets includes Casella, an Australian bulk wine producer, which partnered with Deutsch, a New York-based wine importer, to develop and market the Yellowtail wine brand.

Alliances and partnerships have their pitfalls. It is not unusual for partners to discover they have conflicting objectives and strategies, deep differences of opinion about how to proceed, or important differences in corporate values and ethical standards. Tensions build, working relationships cool, and the hoped-for benefits never materialize. In those respects, business partnerships may seem hauntingly similar to your personal friendships or even romantic relationships.

One of the most notable examples of a failed cross-border partnership was that of Royal Dutch Shell, a petroleum company based in Holland, and Lego, a Danish toy company. In July 2014, Greenpeace released a widely watched and shared YouTube video that criticized the partnership by enveloping a picturesque LEGO arctic construction with thick, unforgiving crude oil…all to a melancholy rendition of *The Lego Movie* theme, "Everything is NOT Awesome." [To watch, see: https://www.youtube.com/watch?v=CM_HFLIsaKo]. The two companies' partnership ended in October 2014.

In sum, partnerships and alliances can be used to determine what is most important for competing globally, in that it can help strategists to:

1. Predict where foreign entrants into an industry are most likely to come from;
2. Prepare to cope with new foreign competitors according to rivals' strengths;
3. Reveal those countries in which foreign rivals are likely to be weakest to help managers decide which foreign markets to enter first; and

4. Further their understanding of the advantages and drawbacks of conducting particular business activities in that country.

Urban Style should be aware that fierce competitive conditions in its home U.S. market for fashion streetwear is not entirely a deal-killer, since facing and overcoming home rivalry should toughen the business and prepare the company for competing internationally. There are, however, two "wild cards" that it must contend with when competing across borders. First, there is a risk of a major political shift toward nationalization of all enterprises or selected industries due to government action. Second, there is a risk of adverse shifts in currency exchange rates that cause purchasing power to grow or shrink. For companies that are risk-averse, two additional strategies are available: licensing and franchising. These are sometimes referred to as "staying local but acting global strategies."

Staying Local but Acting Global Strategies

Operating domestic plants as a production base for exporting Urban Style's clothing products to foreign markets can be an excellent initial strategy for pursuing international sales. It is a conservative way to "test the international waters." The amount of capital needed to begin exporting is often minimal; existing production capacity may well be sufficient to make goods for export. Using an export-based entry strategy, a manufacturer can limit its involvement in foreign markets by contracting with foreign wholesalers who have experience in importing to handle the entire distribution and marketing function in their countries or regions of the world. If it is more advantageous to maintain control over these functions, however, a manufacturer can establish its own distribution and sales organizations in some or all of the target foreign markets, via licensing and franchising agreements.

Licensing. as an entry strategy for Urban Style makes sense but only if it has already established valuable technical know-how, an appealing brand, or a unique patented product has neither the internal organizational capability nor the resources to enter foreign markets. Licensing has the advantage of avoiding the risks of committing resources to country markets that are unfamiliar, politically volatile, economically unstable, or otherwise risky. By licensing the technology, trademark, or production rights to foreign-based companies, the firm can generate income from royalties while shifting the costs and risks of entering foreign markets to the licensee.

For example, the Walt Disney Company has become largest licensor of its brands worldwide: merchandise, media, theme parks, toys, and movies including the Disney pictures, Pixar, Star Wars, and Marvel Universe.

While licensing works well for manufacturers and owners of proprietary technology, however, franchising is often better suited to the international expansion efforts of service and retailing enterprises.

Franchising. has many of the same advantages as licensing, particularly on the retail side of the fashion business equation. A franchisee bears most of the costs and risks of establishing foreign locations for Urban Style, whereas Urban Style has to expend only the resources to recruit, train, support, and monitor franchisees. To use location to build a competitive advantage using franchising, a company must consider two issues: (a) whether to concentrate each activity it performs in a few select countries or to disperse performance of the activity to many nations, and (b) in which countries to locate particular activities.

For example, Domino's Pizza was founded in 1960 and by 2021 extended its reach via franchising to over 85 countries, with almost 17,100 stores, of which nearly11,000 are international franchisees.

To sum up, the two basic "think local, act global" strategy options for local companies like Urban Style in competing against global challengers include licensing and franchising. Three major factors shape a company's strategic approach if it has decided to compete in foreign markets: (a) The degree to which there are important cross-country differences in demographic, cultural, and market conditions; (b) whether opportunities exist to gain a location-based advantage based on wage rates, worker productivity, inflation rates, energy costs, tax rates, and other factors that impact cost structure; and (c) the extent to which governmental policies affect the local business climate.

Globalization is built around the flow of manufactured goods, services, people, and capital across borders. A global shock like COVID or political instability abroad disrupts these flows—and provides an opportunity for businesses like Urban Style to reconsider whether or not globalization is the right way to proceed with diversifying its production and/or consumer base(s) (Costa, 2022).

De-Globalization

Debates regarding the benefits and limits of globalization have traditionally focused on how businesses need to develop dynamic capabilities to compete successfully, and conversely, the longer-term prospects for de-globalization (Williamson, 2021; Zahra et al., 2022). Witt et al. (2021: 6–7) posit that most companies today profess that they care about acting in socially responsible ways. With reference to how Western businesses have become reliant on China, for example, the authors ask:

1. How much are Western societies willing to pay to preserve their way of life?
2. Is it ethical or socially responsible to exploit regulatory loopholes to circumvent restrictions on doing business with Chinese companies?
3. How likely is it that other countries' high-tech firms will stand a chance against Chinese competitors in the medium- to long-term without state protection and support?
4. Might decoupling from a dependence on China for low-cost manufacturing and potentially enormous consumer markets save, rather than doom, Western companies?

Emerging technological revolutions affect manufacturing (e.g., artificial intelligence or AI, three-dimensional printing, robotics, and digital transformation) as well as the reorganization of business sectors, such as hospitality, retail, fintech, and the sharing economy (e.g., Uber and the gig economy). These technological innovations have not yet, at least as of this writing, been completely perfected and brought to market, however (Ciravegna & Michaelova, 2022). There are three compelling reasons why we can expect de-globalization, in response to the pandemic, climate change, and other societal shocks to be a slow process, at best (Williamson (2021): Re-shoring and re-localizing production may not significantly improve supply chain efficiencies; comparative advantages could evaporate on both the cost reduction (supply) and the revenue enhancement (demand) sides; and innovation necessitates identification of and access to specialist knowledge and capabilities that are already scattered around the world.

Limited improvement of supply chain efficiencies. A supply chain relying solely on limited local capacity hampered by a local lockdown or power outages or even military conflicts would be unable to quickly increase production to meet rapid spikes in demand. Following regulatory approval of a test kit for COVID-19, for example, Korea was able to increase production of test kits to one million per week within one month and three million per week within 45 days, with 90 percent available for export. This was possible in large part because Korea was already producing in-vitro diagnostics products at large scale prior to the COVID-19 crisis (Kim et al., 2020).

Evaporation of comparative advantages. Multinational enterprises are reluctant to surrender the potential to grow their sales, particularly in emerging markets such as Brazil, Russia, India, and China). These promising markets would be difficult to enter as a result of de-globalization. China, for example, is already the largest market for many products from commodities, such as pork and eggs, to luxury goods, such as automobiles and cosmetics products. It is unlikely that Western multinationals, many now heavily indebted as a result of losses associated with COVID-19, will choose to invest in re-shoring and localized production when the growth in demand for their products and services is almost solely in emerging markets such as China.

Loss of access to specialist knowledge around the world. A Boston Consulting Group study in March 2020 concluded that de-globalization of the semiconductor industry would result in severe cuts in R&D and capital expenditures by multinationals, and the loss of 15,000 to 40,000 highly skilled direct jobs in the U.S. semiconductor industry. Moreover, the development of vaccines for COVID-19 has been disbursed around the globe to companies in China, Germany, India, Russia, Sweden, U.K., and U.S. (Klobucista, 2022). Pfizer-BioNTech's COVID-19 vaccine was, as of January 2022, produced among 11 sites across five countries, including the U.S., Germany, Belgium, Ireland, and Croatia, and engages more than 20 suppliers.

Tradeoffs in Changing Supply Chains

Regardless of the forces of geopolitics or the desire of executives to increase their perceived control by re-localizing supply or bringing it in-house, the costs of doing so can be prohibitive—and may also result in the closure of consumer markets by governments in countries where goods and services are produced, i.e., due to local content laws. For example, moving iPhone production out of China could cost Apple as much as 30 percent in increased production costs and a potential loss of customers, as Apple's share of the mobile phone market in China reached 23 percent in the fourth quarter of 2021 (Kelly, 2022; Rathke & O'Connell, 2020).

We now turn to how a small company like Urban Style can make globalization work. Globalization might help companies like Urban Style to achieve the original promise of raising all boats in rich and poor countries alike and deterring the existential threats to society thought to be posed by climate change, weaponized pandemics, nuclear war, and uber-powerful AI (Macaskill, 2022). That said, this benefit has not yet materialized as evidenced by displaced employees in rich countries and claims of social injustice, unfair working conditions, and environmental mismanagement by multinational corporations in poor countries.

Why Strategists Need to Be Forward-Looking

Global strategy-making is more than simply thinking about the future of a business like Urban Style outside of its home market. Companies also need to focus on future customer-market needs, including those that their customers may not yet have identified for themselves. As discussed earlier in Chapter 2, developing one's strategic foresight is critical in determining where to place bets globally as well as in technology.

Strategic foresight is said to be the ability to anticipate discontinuities in the business environment, the threats and opportunities to the enterprise, as well as any impending disruptive moves to be made by competitors (Custis, 2012).

We will take up the interplay between technology and strategy in the next chapter.

End of Chapter Mini-Case: E.L.F. Beauty, Inc. Faces Global Supply Chain Decisions

Michelle Parrish

In March 2022, Tarang Amin, Chairman of the Board, President, and Chief Executive Officer of e.l.f. Beauty Inc. (e.l.f) pondered how his cosmetics business could sustain supply chain operations despite

M. Parrish
Sonoma State University, Rohnert Park, CA, USA

mounting political, environmental, and economic challenges. e.l.f. (short for EyesLipsFace) solely sourced and manufactured its products from China, a nation that also represented nearly 10 percent of the company's consumer sales. The company was founded in 2004.

Because e.l.f. contracted with third-party logistics operators and suppliers to source, manufacture, deliver, and retail its cosmetics products, the company also had to contend with rapidly rising fuel prices and transportation costs in the first half of 2022, partly as a result of Russia's invasion into Ukraine. Pressures to increase prices continued to mount.

Amin identified four potential options: (1) be patient and await the restoration of normal supply lines and wait times with the company's current Chinese manufacturing partners; (2) re-shore manufacturing to the U.S., (3) manufacture closer to the U.S. (also known as "nearshoring") by relocating production to Mexico, or (4) regionalize by setting up multiple factories that could reduce the risk associated with having products manufactured in a single country location.

The company's four major product lines included e.l.f. Cosmetics, e.l.f. Skin, W3LL PEOPLE, and KEYS SoulCare, the latter a lifestyle beauty brand created by recording artist, producer, actress, and best-selling author Alicia Keys. e.l.f. utilized an "omnichannel" distribution strategy whereby customers could shop online from a desktop, mobile device, or in a brick-and-mortar store. An omnichannel strategy was a multichannel approach to sales to provide customers with a seamless shopping experience, whether they were shopping online from a desktop or mobile device, by telephone, or in a brick-and-mortar store.

e.l.f also sold products online through its direct e-commerce channels and via national retailers in the U.S., such as Target, Walmart, and Ulta Beauty. To serve its primary U.S. markets, e.l.f. operated two main distribution centers: one in Ontario, California, which mainly served U.S. retail customers, and an e-commerce distribution center in Columbus, Ohio.

International markets included Canada, China, Germany, Italy, and the U.K. All told, e.l.f. posted $318 million in sales in fiscal 2021, an increase of 12 percent over 2020. See Fig. 7.1 for information on e.l.f. Beauty's domestic and international operating results, tabulating the company's net sales revenues from 2018 to 2021.

The March 2020 onset of the COVID-19 pandemic disrupted numerous global supply chains, causing massive backlogs and shortages which led many U.S. companies dependent on offshore suppliers to re-evaluate their location strategies to protect their supply chains and bottom

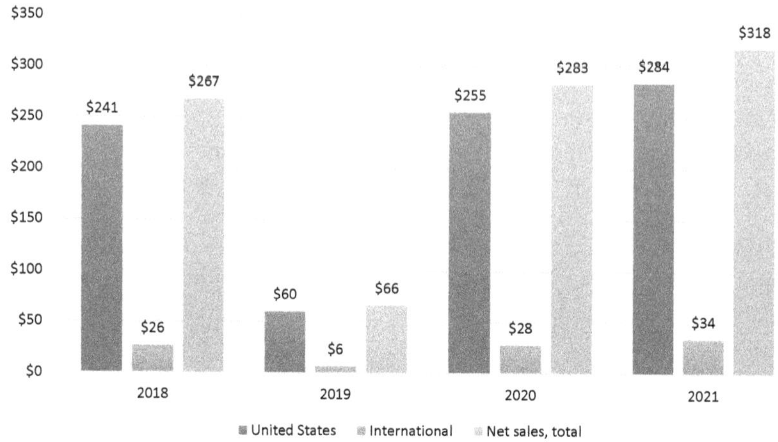

Fig. 7.1 e.l.f. Beauty, Inc., Net Sales by Region, 2018–2021 ($ millions) (*Note* Fiscal year 2019 represented a transition period for e.l.f. Beauty due to the change of fiscal year end from 12/31 to 3/31 in 2019. *Source* e.l.f Beauty, Inc. [2021]. Form 10-K. Retrieved November 11, 2021, from: https://www.marketwatch.com/investing/secfile/14993723)

lines. Consumers also had to adapt to intermittent supply shortages and increases in prices. Two years later, consumers and companies were still grappling with the supply chain challenges. In 2021, the cost of shipping increased, inducing e.l.f. to pass along those increases by raising the prices of its products. Consumers switched to other brands due to e.l.f.'s stock-outs online and at brick-and-mortar retailers.

Industry-wide, there were 124 contract manufacturers of cosmetics in the U.S., eight in Canada, and five in China as of October 2021. China exported nearly one million metric tons of cosmetics and personal care products in 2020, valued at around $4.2 billion. All foreign companies doing business in China faced risks from that nation's growing tensions with Taiwan, as well as political, legal, and economic issues such as taxation, inflation, import and export tariffs, and energy and labor shortages. Compounding the challenges for consumers, annualized inflation rates in the U.S. steeply accelerated to 8.5 percent in March 2022, the nation's highest level since December, 1981.

Quality control and regulatory compliance represented other major risks for the cosmetics company. In 2019, e.l.f. had imported 156 shipments of false eyelash kits, valued at $4.43 million, from two suppliers located in China, and those eyelash kits contained materials the Chinese suppliers had, in turn, sourced from North Korea. e.l.f. had to pay nearly $1 million to settle liabilities for violations of U.S. sanctions barring trading with North Korea.

On November 4, 2021, Amin agreed to be interviewed by "Closing Bell" on CNBC, to discuss the company's latest earnings report as well as its supply chain and pricing challenges. When asked if the company would raise prices due to the issues associated with the supply chain, Amin said:

> We definitely have pricing power. We took one round of pricing earlier this year in May and saw good results. I think it benefited our gross margins by about 100 basis points in this quarter, but as you say, we offer an extraordinary value. While the brand has pricing power, we want to wait a little bit longer to see how many of these costs are permanent in nature or more temporal and then we'll decide but we have pricing power if that's a lever we need to pull.

On the demand side, the value of the global cosmetics market reached $603 billion in 2021, and was projected to grow at an annual rate of 6.2 percent to reach $758.4 billion in 2025. The U.S. cosmetics market was estimated at $14.8 billion and forecasted to grow at a compound annual rate of almost five percent, to $21.9 billion in 2026.

In the European Union (EU), Germany led the market in 2020, purchasing nearly €14 billion worth of cosmetics products, followed by France at €11 billion, and the U.K. at €9.8 billion. Significant growth in EU markets was forecast by cosmetics industry analysts from 2021–2028, contingent on supply availability, inflationary pressures, the potential for recessions, and the state of the war between Russia and Ukraine.

Beauty and personal care products in China were also forecasted to grow from $51.8 billion in 2020 to $78.5 billion in 2025.

In the years following the onset of the COVID-19 pandemic in 2020, consumer preferences around the globe began to shift in favor of natural and organic color cosmetics, in part due to social media-driven awareness of the toxic ingredients in synthetic personal care products. Industry analysts predicted that the global market value for natural cosmetics and personal care would witness an annual growth rate of over six percent, from almost $34.5 billion in 2018 to nearly $54.5 billion by 2027.

As CEO Amin considered his options in April 2022, he was well aware that sourcing and manufacturing solely in China could pose ongoing obstacles in e.l.f.'s supply chain. All of these factors could negatively impact the company's financial performance in fiscal 2022 and beyond, resulting in higher inventory costs, reduced sales, and decreasing cash flow. Finally, any attempt to exit from China or diversify its product manufacturing to other locations might impede e.l.f.'s sales to Chinese consumers, an important market.

Lessons learned. The development of international trade is driven by international logistics and management and the provision of the global supply chain. The ultimate objective of global supply chain management is to link the marketplace, distribution network, manufacturing/processing/assembly process, and procurement activity in such a way that customers are serviced at a higher level yet lower cost (Branch, 2009). Resourceful companies like e.l.f. Beauty must successfully manage the entire supply flow, from the sources of the firm, through the value-added processes of the firm, and on to the customers of the firm (Robert & Chase, 2018). This is an opportunity for e.l.f. to improve its operational techniques and reduce production costs. e.l.f. Beauty appears to have outsourced significant portions of its distribution process, as well as certain technology-related functions, to third-party service providers. Revamping e.l.f.'s entire supply chain to select suppliers and manage risk using automated technologies such as artificial intelligence (AI) and virtual reality (VR) will require time and training, but this strategy could pay dividends in the future (Aggarwal & Davé, 2019; Baryannis, et al., 2019). Sophisticated technology adoption in operations and supply chain management will require a new breed of computer literate management that also possesses an acute awareness of the global information technology infrastructure (Roberts, 2018).

Why? Because global supply chains and supporting information technologies connect the world in intricate ways. Despite their dramatic expansion as distinct, complex, and unique mechanisms of economic interdependence, the role of supply chains in broader patterns of interstate conflict and cooperation has been relatively neglected (Solingen, 2021; Zahra et al., 2022). For example, can a highly interdependent "Factory Asia" and Asia–Pacific withstand geopolitical, geo-economic, and pandemic threats? This combustible mix, fueled by rising hyper-nationalism in the U.S. and China, threatens to unleash sizable disruptions in the global geography of production and in the international relations of East Asia (Solingen, 2021).

End of Chapter Strategic Planning Exercise

Where Does it Come From?

Make a written inventory of all of the consumer products in your medicine cabinet, vanity drawer, wardrobe, kitchen pantry, or on your desk. Read the labels. Create a table that lists where these products were manufactured or sourced.

Then, write a summary paragraph that answers the following questions: Would knowing their original source(s) have made a difference in your initial purchase decision? Why or why not? Supposing supply chain shortages prevented you from purchasing these products again. What would you do? Would you switch to a locally-sourced product?

Further Reading

Aggarwal, A. K., & Davè, D. S. (2019). Supplier selection in supply chains: A SWOT guided artificial intelligence approach. *IUP Journal of Supply Chain Management, 16*(3), 27–35.

Bartlett, C. A., & Ghoshal, S. (1989). *Managing across borders: The transnational solution*. Harvard Business School Press.

Baryannis, G., Validi, S., Dani, S., & Antoniou, G. (2019). Supply chain risk management and artificial intelligence: State of the art and future research directions. *International Journal of Production Research, 57*(7), 2179–2202.

Branch, A. E. (2009). *Global supply chain management and international logistics*. Routledge.

Carroll, A. B. (2004). Managing ethically with global stakeholders: A present and future challenge. *Academy of Management Executive, 18*(2), 114–120.

Ciravegna, L., & Michailova, S. (2022). Why the world economy needs, but will not get, more globalization in the post-COVID-19 decade. *Journal of International Business Studies, 53*, 172–186.

Costa, J. (2022). Internationalization strategies at a crossroads: Family business market diffusion in the post-COVID era. *Economies, 10*(7), N.PAG. https://doi.org/10.3390/economies10070170

Custis, C. (2012). The role of business intelligence within the hospitality industry's information systems strategy: Historical concepts and future trends. *Journal of Management Policy and Practice, 13*(3), 82–94.

Gentile, M. C. (2016). Talking about ethics across cultures. *Harvard Business Review Digital Articles*, 2–4. Accessed January 30, 2023.

Hill, C. W. L. & Jones, G. R. (2004). *Strategic management: An integrated approach, 6/E*. Houghton Mifflin, Chapter 8, "Strategy in the Global Environment."

Kelly, S. (2022, February 24). Apple reaches highest-ever market share in China. *Swrve*. Retrieved August 15, 2022 from: https://www.swrve.com/resources/weblog/apple-reaches-highest-ever-market-share-in-china#:~:text=Apple's%20smartphone%20market%20share%20in,the%20fourth%20quarter%20of%202021

Kim, B-h., Kim, S-g., & Kim, M. (2020, April 9). Korean-made COVID-19 testing kits demanded by over 100 countries. *Maeil Business News Korea*. Retrieved August 15, 2022, from: https://pulsenews.co.kr/view.php?year=2020&no=374050

Klobucista, C. (2022, July 19). A guide to global COVID-19 vaccine efforts. *Council on Foreign Relations*. Retrieved August 15, 2022 from: https://www.cfr.org/backgrounder/guide-global-covid-19-vaccine-efforts#chapter-title-0-5

Macaskill, W. (2022, August 15). *What we owe the future*. Zoom webinar and book preview presented by The Harvard Club of New York City.

Melanie, P. L., Jase, R. R., & James "Mick" Andzulis, & George, R. F. (2020). The dark side of cultural intelligence: Exploring its impact on opportunism, ethical relativism, and customer relationship performance. *Business Ethics Quarterly, 30*(4), 552–590.

Porter, M. E. (1990). *The competitive advantage of nations*. Free Press.

Rathke, S. & O'Connell, J. E. (2020), April 30. Global supply chains in the wake of COVID-19 in socially critical industries—Is it time to reshore? *Lexology*. Retrieved August 15, 2022 from: https://www.lexology.com/library/detail.aspx?g=40c6d60a-2794-44ec-8311-27b1649f9962

Robert, J. F., & Chase, R. B. (2018). *Operations and supply chain management*. John Wiley & Sons.

Solingen, E. (2021). *Geopolitics, supply chains, and international relations in East Asia*. Cambridge University Press.

Teargarden, M. (2021). Are we on the road to de-globalization? Letter from the Editor. *Thunderbird International Business Review, 64*(3). https://doi.org/10.1002/tie.22245

Valentine, S. R., & Bateman, C. R. (2011). The impact of ethical ideologies, moral intensity, and social context on sales-based ethical reasoning. *Journal of Business Ethics, 102*(1), 155–168.

Wang, L. C., & Calvano, L. (2015). Is business ethics education effective? An analysis of gender, personal ethical perspectives, and moral judgment. *Journal of Business Ethics, 126*(4), 591–602.

Williamson, P. (2021). De-globalisation and decoupling: Post-COVID-19 myths versus realities. *Management & Organization Review, 17*(1), 29–34. https://doi.org/10.1017/mor.2020.80

Witt, M., Li, P. P., Valikangas, L., & Lewin, A. (2021). De-globalization and de-coupling: Game changing consequences? *Management and Organization Review, 17*(1), 6–15.

Zahra, S. A., Petricevic, O., & Luo, Y. (2022). Toward an action-based view of dynamic capabilities for international business. *Journal of International Business Studies, 53*(4), 583–600. https://doi.org/10.1057/s41267-021-00487-2

CHAPTER 8

Innovation and the Changing Workplace

Abstract In this chapter, you will learn how technological innovations are changing the workplace.

Keywords Technologies: base · key · and pacing · Innovation · Remote and hybrid workplaces · Workplace monitoring

Introduction

The major challenges in developing and sustaining a competitive strategy in any era relate to the need to strike a balance between sudden and unexpected external market pressures, such as societal shocks, and long-term planning. The goal is to sustain rapid growth in the face of how those shocks may in time reshape the norms of work.

To be successful, Carol Dweck, a Stanford researcher, writes: "growth-mindset companies have happier employees and a more innovative, risk-taking culture" (Dweck, 2014). As we observed in the previous chapter, today many innovative businesses are pursuing globalization to rein in labor and production costs while expanding their geographic reach to capture new customers. A well-known example of a global manufacturer and marketer is Apple, Inc.

A. Gilinsky, *Business Strategy for a Better Normal*,
https://doi.org/10.1007/978-3-031-28708-4_8

Other organizations are foregoing globalization, trying to preserve their traditional business models that include a high-quality brand image, hands-on, caring cultures, and commitment to DEI, highlighted previously in Chapter 6. An employee-owned corporation, King Arthur Baking, primarily known for King Arthur flour, is America's oldest flour company and premier baking resource and has been in business since 1790.

In general, however, "[the early 2020s] have been a period of surprises for business leaders—they don't know where their employees are working," or even if they are more or less productive remotely or in the office (Goldberg, 2022b: BU5). While remaining socially distant, many workers and students have missed the established work routines and the unplanned interactions that can result in better teamwork and more creative thinking (Ciravegna & Michailova, 2022). Yet many companies are fearful of losing out on talent and productivity because their competitors are embracing more flexibility in terms of office work (Kantor & Sundaram, 2022).

The Remoteness of Things

With respect to growth, innovation, or even risk-taking, there is still much to be learned regarding the workplace. There are unknown benefits and limitations of working remotely, or even of making a hybrid work commitment, and returning to the office (Jeske, 2021). Some of the pros and cons of remote work include (Chan et al., 2007):

Pros

- Reduces overhead costs—a boon in competitive, fast-paced organizational environment of globalization.
- Provides agility companies need to adjust to the changing needs of the global business environment.
- Offsets rising costs of transportation, social changes in work-life tension, decline in the norms of close supervision, and growing desire for employees' independence are all conditions that favor the self-management of remote work.
- Increases ease of entry and setup while decreasing real estate allocated per worker.

Cons

- Not all organizations are suited to a virtual/remote workplace strategy.
- Fosters feelings of isolation and mistrust that may quickly erode any social capital that may form the critical competitive edge of the organization.
- Depletes "emotional capital" or necessary trust that is built up between individuals only through face-to-face meetings, which is then expended in remote conversations.
- Precludes creative workplace design solutions emphasizing flexibility and short-term team formation,
- Ignores the reality that some work simply cannot be performed in a virtual/remote setup.
- Presents barriers to formal and informal communication, e.g., conflict resolution in the workplace requires face-to-face mitigation, and chance conversations and meetings that are valued by the organization are unlikely to occur.

Innovation and risk-taking have also changed the workplace, partly in response to societal shocks. World events from 2020–2022 highlighted that most countries were ready to adopt measures halting globalization and technology diffusion for national security reasons. The workplace, after all, is dominated by people, or human assets. Human assets provide intellectual capital, unplanned interactions, the know-how of specialized teams and work groups; knowledge of key personnel concerning important business functions (e.g., skills in keeping operating costs low, improving product quality, and providing customer service); managerial talent; and the creativity and innovativeness of fellow personnel (Pisano, 2015).

Is the success of a business solely contingent upon having its human assets together in a room, or can modern technology bridge that gap? (Goldberg, 2021; Goldberg, 2022a).

For example, have technological innovations—such as Zoom meetings, shared workspaces in the cloud for collaborating on documents and spreadsheets, digital wallets, apps to make transactions, and fitness trackers to maintain health—kept people apart or brought us together, reduced isolation and loneliness, much less helped with workplace mentoring and career advancement? (Purtill, 2022).

Three Types of Technology

Technology is the application of scientific knowledge for practical use in businesses. That knowledge may be from the applied sciences such as biological, chemical, engineering, and mechanical. Technology is an important distinctive competency for businesses. Technologies may be classified as base, key, and pacing (María & Díaz-Garrido 2008).

Base technologies. These are generally considered as applications of science and engineering that are considered to be readily available to businesses and consumers for everyday use. Base technologies are used in home appliances, automobiles, televisions, communications devices, generic pharmaceuticals, medical equipment, recording/playback machines, electronic game consoles, and personal computers.

Key technologies. Businesses are always seeking a competitive edge, and may achieve this via the adoption of what are known as key technologies, which are also considered valued and vital to sustainability and growth. Examples of key information and production technologies include artificial intelligence (AI), augmented reality, cloud computing, computer security, computer software to handle and analyze large data sets, customer relationship management systems (CRM), the Internet of things (via connections of everyday devices to WiFi networks), nanotechnology, radiology, robotics, and power generation alternatives (geothermal, solar, wind, and fuel cells).

Artificial Intelligence, for example, is the technology used to drive Alexa, Siri, Amazon's product recommendations, Netflix's and Spotify's personalized recommendations, every Google search you make, facial recognition, self-driving cars, security checks for fraudulent credit card purchases, dating apps, fitness trackers, and the like.

Do you or someone you know enjoy beer? Savvy craft breweries, like Delirium in Belgium, are increasingly turning to intelligent automation to increase productivity, flexibility, and profits. Adopting robotics in keg picking and packing applications, for example, can reap multiple benefits for breweries seeking to lower costs by replacing human labor, increase production, and improve quality control for product consistency. For smaller craft breweries robotics can offer the opportunity to scale up operations to reach a wider pool of consumers. One of the first craft beers created by AI was Toronto, Canada's Kensington Brewing Company's A Little Robotics, which is a smoothie style double dry-hopped IPA that consists of mango puree and lactose.

Pacing technologies. Long-range planning involves identifying, understanding, and being prepared to adopt the technologies of the future. These are known as pacing technologies, and some may overlap with the key technologies discussed earlier. Examples of pacing technologies include advanced materials (such as ceramics and composites of metals and plastic), 3D printing, extended reality (XR), genomics, life support systems, and machine learning, to name a few.

Using 3D printing, the factories of the future could quickly print spare parts for machinery on site. Entire assembly lines could be replaced with 3D printers. We could print human tissue for transplant, weapons, and even food. Extended Reality encompasses virtual reality, augmented reality, and mixed reality and refers to the use of technology to create more immersive digital experiences as well as improved human–computer interfaces.

Genomics, a subset of the field of biotechnology, has been advancing to the point where it's viable to alter the DNA encoded within a cell; this will influence the characteristics or traits that its descendants will have. In plants, this could affect the number of leaves or their coloring, while in humans, it could affect their height, eye color, or their likelihood of developing diseases.

The Dark Sides of Technology and the Changing Workplace

Lack of trust has been the biggest holdback to telework or remote work since the term was coined in 1972. Supporters of employee-monitoring systems tout productivity enhancement tools aimed at helping people avoid distractions (Forman et al., 2014).

More than 60% of employers have purchased and implemented employee-monitoring software since the start of the pandemic, with the number expected to rise to 70% by 2025 (Gartner, 2022). Employee-monitoring software includes tools that track keystrokes; log software and Web activity; and record audio, video and electronic communications—and they're decidedly unsuitable in an age when brains, not brawn, are the means to production. Who is tracking what? A number of companies have developed technologies for employee monitoring, as shown in Table 8.1.

Table 8.1 Monitoring software: Developers and vendors

Company	*Email response time*	*Log on/off times*	*Time on social media*	*Keyboard/ mouse activity*	*Webcam*	*Email content*	*Keyword alerts*	*Employees might be unaware*
ActivTrack		✓	✓	✓				✓
Enaible	✓	✓	✓					✓
Hubstaff			✓	✓				
InterGuard		✓	✓	✓				✓
Monitask		✓	✓	✓				✓
Sneek					✓			✓
Teramind	✓	✓	✓	✓		✓	✓	
TimeCamp		✓	✓	✓		✓	✓	

Source Adapted and updated from data provided by Hunter (2021), Crunchbase, and company websites

Some might well ask, "why do managers receive the data rather than employees? What is so bad about occasional distractions?"

Daron Acemoglu, a researcher from MIT, wrote to a *New York Times* opinion writer in November 2022, "Robotics and artificial intelligence (AI) are also impacting the workplace. and forthcoming digital technologies such as augmented reality and machine learning are likely to have an even bigger impact. This is both via automation and worker surveillance. Digital technologies are being increasingly used to monitor workers closely and impose worse working arrangements on them" (Edsall, 2022).

If surveillance tools have any role in the organization, such as for ensuring data security or employee safety as they have been used in the past, they should be deployed in ways that are laser-focused on those purposes and available to a limited few (Ambalavanan & Lister, 2020). Monitoring productivity is vastly more complicated, at least from an ethical standpoint. Some researchers have observed that the increasing adoption and deployment of information technology has opened up this Pandora's Box (Starbuck & Mezias, 1996).

End of Chapter Mini-Case: Blue Apron

Kayla Kremer

Founded in New York in 2012, Blue Apron was an e-commerce meal-kit service that delivered pre-portioned ingredients and recipe guidelines for subscribers to cook at home. Blue Apron also sold wine and cooking accessories. Since filing for an IPO in 2017, the company struggled to maintain its initial success, resulting in a then record-low stock price on March 13, 2020.

One day after the U.S. observed its first stay-at-home order due to the onset of the COVID-19 pandemic on March 19, 2020, Blue Apron's stock increased 345%. This was followed by several profitable quarters due to changing consumer buying behaviors.

Blue Apron's key rivals, Hello Fresh, Home Chef, Sunbasket, and Plated also enjoyed modest benefits from the stay-at-home, eat-at-home trend that continued throughout 2020 and for most of the first half of 2021.

External Innovation

In December 2020, a team of Master's students in a design competition at Carnegie Mellon University won first prize when it created Chef, a conversational assistant in the kitchen to facilitate personalized, hands-free interactions while preparing food. While guiding the user throughout the cooking process, Chef was designed to make the culinary experience more accessible and enjoyable. Accessible on Blue Apron's mobile app and a smart home display, Chef's capabilities in and out of the kitchen included:

- Making personalized meal recommendations based on user preference,
- connecting to smart kitchen devices for a streamlined cooking experience,
- guiding individuals and multiple users through the cooking experience,

K. Kremer
Sonoma State University, Rohnert Park, CA, USA

- providing ingredient substitutions in real-time,
- keeping track of multiple timers, and
- integrating with third-party applications like MyFitnessPal, Spotify, and YouTube.

Although Blue Apron did not immediately acknowledge the Carnegie Mellon student team's technology, in December 2021, Blue Apron added ordering and recipe retrieval to Alexa. In an effort to lower long-term costs and to increase scalability, the company also began making investments in more efficient machinery.

Pivot and Pushback

Despite employees' preferences to work from home, the gradual return to work in late 2021 and early 2022, coupled with changing purchasing habits in ordering prepared meals from e-commerce delivery vendors such as GrubHub and DoorDash, put downward pressure on Blue Apron's revenues and profits.

In response, Blue Apron loosened its subscription requirements and entered into strategic partnerships with Amazon, Panasonic, Walmart, and The Knot. Management hoped that Blue Apron's partnerships would result in greater demand from a post-pandemic customer base.

Changing Fortunes

In an early 2022 interview Blue Apron's CEO Linda Findley stated that improvements to its fulfillment centers such as increased line speed, overall utilization, and machine optimization solved some of the company's labor shortage issues that had been caused by the pandemic. The company had 2,343 employees as of October 2022. On November 3, 2022, Blue Apron's stock price was at the lowest in the company's history, less than a week in advance of the company's public release of its results for the third quarter of 2022.

Lesson learned. A big hurdle for businesses, then, is how to link technology and innovation to the primary core values that form their operating systems. Every organization needs a strategy that defines boundaries but also allows for personal freedoms (Hunter, 2021). Clarifying what is in and what is out of bounds ensures that experimentation is not rampant and is encouraged within those parameters. Boundaries help businesses identify the long-term attractiveness of technology and the potential impacts on suppliers, workers, and customers before testing their feasibility. By combining strategy and experimentation in such a fashion, all companies can greatly increase the odds of achieving lasting success (Collis, 2016: 68).

So, consider providing your business with some easy-to-understand boundaries within which innovation can thrive. After all, the executive team that is responsible for implementing your recommended strategy—you are surely considering ways to improve your businesses, aren't you?—needs to know how to assess accurately whether its planned investments in people and technology are likely to generate returns that exceed their costs over time, not to mention the unforeseen ethical dilemmas that may well arise after making those investments.

End of Chapters Strategic Planning Exercises

Choosing Technology

You have been hired by CEO Tracy Montgomery as a consultant to Fresco, a family-owned wholesale food distribution company (names and locations disguised), which is facing stiff competition from larger integrated food distributors such as Sysco, U.S. Foods, and McLane Foodservice.

Founded in 1992, Fresco, based in Nutley, New Jersey, reached $8 billion in sales and $215 million in profits in 2022, had 2,000 employees, and operated 11 distribution hubs nationwide, in addition to its headquarters. The company had a stated commitment to diversity and the well-being of its people, embodied in its mission statement, "Fresco Cares."

While interviewing Fresco's management and staff, you learned that:

- Fresco owns a fleet of older gasoline-powered trucks that feature last generation refrigeration technology.
- Fresco's office staff spends a good amount of time waiting on legacy tools used to get work done, because the company's CRM software, e-mail clients, landline phones, and printers have not been updated in ten years.

- Fresco has missed its sales targets for the two most recent consecutive quarters, and management is not only reluctant to make any new investments, but has also instituted a hiring freeze.

What should Fresco do now to achieve long term success? Which key and/or pacing technology(ies) would you recommend to Fresco? For example, would investments in autonomous (self-driving) electric trucks and the "Internet of things" be worth making?

Create a table of options and pros and cons of each that demonstrate whether or not Fresco should invest in innovative technologies, noting the potential downsides of any new technology chosen.

Further Reading

Ambalavanan, B., & Lister, K. (2020). Should employers use software to monitor remote workers? *HR Magazine, 65*(3), 30–31.

Chan, J. K., Beckman, S. L., & Lawrence, P. G. (2007). Workplace design: A new managerial imperative. *California Management Review, 49*(2), 6–22.

Ciravegna, L., & Michailova, S. (2022). Why the world economy needs, but will not get, more globalization in the post-COVID-19 decade. *Journal of International Business Studies, 53*, 172–186.

Collis, D. (2016). Lean strategy. *Harvard Business Review, 94*(3), 62–68.

Dweck, C. (2014, November). How companies can prosper from a "growth mindset." *Harvard Business Review*, 118–119.

Edsall, T. B. (2022, November 2). 'Elites are making choices that are not good news.' *New York Times.* Retrieved November 3, 2022 from: https://www.nytimes.com/2022/11/02/opinion/artificial-intelligence-automation-jobs-populism.html

Forman, C., King, J. L., & Lyytinen, K. (2014). Information, technology, and the changing nature of work. *Information Systems Research, 25*(4), 789–795.

Gartner (2022, June 9). The right way to monitor employee productivity. Retrieved November 3, 2022 from: https://www.gartner.com/en/articles/the-right-way-to-monitor-your-employee-productivity.

Goldberg, E., (2021, December 11). The new language of the office, from al desko dining to zoombies. *The New York Times.* https://www.nytimes.com/2021/12/11/business/new-corporate-jargon.html

Goldberg, E., (2022a, April 13). A two-year, 50-million-person experiment in changing how we work. *The New York Times.* https://www.nytimes.com/2022a/03/10/business/remote-work-office-life.html

Goldberg, E., (2022b, August 28). The office's last stand. *The New York Times,* BU1. https://www.nytimes.com/2022b/08/28/business/the-offices-last-stand.html?searchResultPosition=1

Hunter, T. (2021, September 24). Here are all the ways your boss can legally monitor you. *The Washington Post*. https://www.washingtonpost.com/technology/2021/08/20/work-from-home-computer-monitoring/

Kantor, J., & Sundaram, A. (2022, August 14). The rise of the worker productivity score. *The New York Times*. https://www.nytimes.com/interactive/2022/08/14/business/worker-productivity-tracking.html?searchResultPosition=3

Jeske, D. (2021). Monitoring remote employees: Implications for HR. *Strategic HR Review, 20*(2), 42–46.

María, L. M., & Díaz-Garrido, E. (2008). Typologies and taxonomies of operations strategy: A literature review. *Management Research News, 31*(3), 200–218.

Pisano, G. P. (2015). You need an innovation strategy. *Harvard Business Review, 93*(6), 44–54.

Purtill, C. (2022, March 10). Can workers climb the career ladder from outside the office? *The New York Times*. https://www.nytimes.com/2022/03/03/business/dealbook/remote-work-careers.html

Starbuck, W. H., & Mezias, J. M. (1996). Opening pandora's box: Studying the accuracy of manager's perceptions. *Journal of Organizational Behavior, 17*, 99–117.

CHAPTER 9

Governance

Abstract In this chapter, you will learn that crafting strategies for the better normal entails having to "begin the process with the end in mind." That is, provide for outstanding organizational governance and oversight to assure continuity to achieve successful, sustainable outcomes.

Keywords Balance · Governance · Leadership · Stakeholders' expectations · Sustainability

Introduction

Decision-making concepts and frameworks discussed in the previous chapters are major topics in the strategic management domain. These concepts and frameworks, as well as the end of chapter mini-cases may have limited shelf lives as strategists strive to attain a better normal.

What does a better normal mean? In a word: balance. Business is just one part of a balanced life. A balanced life may also consist of an emphasis on family, health, lifelong learning, relationships, self-actualization, and spirituality. At certain points in one's life, any of these elements may come to the fore. Whelan and Fink (2016) make note of the fact that twenty-first-century employees are increasingly focusing on mission, purpose,

A. Gilinsky, *Business Strategy for a Better Normal*,
https://doi.org/10.1007/978-3-031-28708-4_9

and work-life balance. The ability or inability to achieve balance impacts successful strategy implementation (Morkel et al., 2021: 36).

The Test of Time

Some strategic leaders intentionally build businesses to sufficiently scale them toward an exit, e.g., via a sale to another company, a private equity or venture capital firm, or initial public offering. Others build businesses to keep and to remain sustainable throughout the generations that will follow. Prior research studies into entrepreneurial and sustainable businesses have seldom tested the impact of governance as a sustainability driver (Golicic et al., 2015). Successive boards of directors and executive teams will be responsible for approving and implementing strategy and surely need to know what is worth preserving from the past and what is worth changing in the future so that their business can stand the test of time.

Governance and Stakeholders

Governance is defined as a company's executive team, which is supported by its board of directors or advisory board (Hitt et al., 2021). Board participation in decision-making extends well beyond arm's length advice-giving (Boivie et al., 2021: 1675). Boards with the expertise and motivation to ask strategically relevant questions during meetings can increase an organization's effectiveness (Boivie et al., 2021: 1686). People who participate in the governance of a business have a responsibility to continuously learn new tools and techniques and also to be responsive to the stakeholders of the organization.

Stakeholders have numerous expectations that vary depending upon perspective. Internal stakeholders include employees and managers. External stakeholders include investors, lenders, customers, suppliers, etc. At least the minimal needs of stakeholders must be satisfied through an organization's actions; otherwise, dissatisfied stakeholders may withdraw their support from the firm and provide it to another organization (Clarkson, 1995), as shown in Table 9.1.

Recent stakeholder theory. Internal and external stakeholders influence changes among different types of intermediary activities (Shane & Venkataraman, 2000). Stakeholder involvement is determined by a

Table 9.1 Managing stakeholders' expectations

Stakeholder	*Stakeholder's expectations*	*If unmet?*
Employees	• Let's work together • We want stable employment and fair compensation • We want to be treated fairly	We can work elsewhere…
Customers	• We want you to meet our needs for quality and safety • We'll both receive value	We can buy elsewhere…
Suppliers	• We want to be paid on time • We want information and repeat business • Let's form an alliance	We can sell elsewhere…
Creditors	• We want principal and interest to be paid back on time	We can seize your assets…
Stockholders/ Investors	• We want you to protect and grow our investment • We want you to become the industry leader	We can withdraw support…
Environment	• Obey the rules • Environment comes first	Mother Nature bats last…
Competitors	• We are all in this together • We can build an industry	We will overtake you…
Government	• We want you to comply with regulations	We can close your operation…
Community	• You have a responsibility	"Not in my backyard"

Source Adapted from Clarkson (1995)

specific organizational mission and goals. Stakeholders are highly influential on an operational as well as strategic level with respect to developing alternative courses of action and playing out the possible problems in implementing those actions (Laur & Danilovic, 2020).

Because stakeholders are so influential when considering the impact of strategic alternatives, there are numerous questions to be answered in order to foster effective governance in organizations (Coulson-Thomas, 2021:24):

- *Organization culture.* Should culture change be the number one priority for boards of directors? Is the composition of the organization's board limiting its ability to embrace change? For example, is there a sufficient diversity of backgrounds and viewpoints to foster cohesion or dissent?

- *Crisis management.* Organizations under pressure and striving to be responsible often face crises, but are those situations viewed as intractable problems or as learning opportunities? For example, are the contributions of executives and outside directors to board discussions based upon strategic thinking or derived from instincts and hunches?
- *Innovation and change.* Many boards are still reluctant to adopt new models of business, governance, operation, organization, and work; is this because of intellectual laziness or a lack of interest? For example, might more than one governance model be required across a diverse enterprise and/or network?
- *DEI and sustainable development.* To what extent are contemporary societal challenges shared? Should people in governance roles focus on challenges facing people and the planet? For example, can the governance of organizations evolve to become a cornerstone of sustainability and responses to existential challenges?
- *Information systems and analytical tools.* Should board members rubber-stamp or challenge the strategies adopted by executive teams? For example, in today's era of "big data," could intelligent scanning, AI, and cognitive systems be combined and harnessed by board members to increase understanding, identify areas that are questionable, and aid in decision-making?
- *Stakeholder engagement.* How should local communities and groups (i.e., chambers of commerce, etc.) be engaged on issues of strategic importance to them? How can organizational governance increase its effectiveness in engaging those stakeholders? For example, how should boards provide the collective responses and collaborative action required to address a global challenge such as climate change?

Non-Market Strategies

Managing relations with government, an important external stakeholder, is often referred to as a "non-market strategy" (Bonardi et al., 2005). Business executives, however, are trained in negotiating markets rather than in negotiating relationships with government relations as the latter is inherently not a market activity, but a political activity (i.e., "lobbying"). Executives who are trained in managing the bottom line may feel uncomfortable with the less precise measures of success in non-market activities such as power and votes and influence rather than dollars and cents (Griener & Lee, 2021). Strategists can ill afford to ignore government and politics, however, because government can have a fundamental impact on the profitability—or lack thereof—of many businesses and industries. Instead, executives should take a proactive approach, making connections with political leaders long before their assistance is needed, since, when a company or industry faces a political crisis, at that point it is likely too late to start political activity to address the problem (Bonardi et al., 2005).

Effective Governance

That said, effective governance does not necessarily correspond to a company having the proper resources to grow profits (Sarros et al., 2002). Gaps between company vision or mission and the resources necessary to carry those out are perceptible if there are incongruent results between the planned and realized strategy (Le & Lei, 2019). Nothing happens if gaps are present. The organization will be in stasis (Soltwisch, 2015).

To make governance a key strength or core competence, organizations need to:

- Establish a clear sense of core values, i.e., purpose and identity, that embraces diversity of backgrounds and viewpoints,
- use information and analysis to question prior assumptions and perceptions of what works,
- foster a culture based on trust that provides a psychologically safe environment for innovation and change, and
- provide for individual and group engagement as well as accountability.

Alternatively, the organization will remain deficient, especially during times of dynamic change or in the face of unforeseen crises (Soltwisch, 2015). The matrix in Fig. 9.1 illustrates one continuum from deficiency to core competence in organizational governance (Luciano et al., 2020).

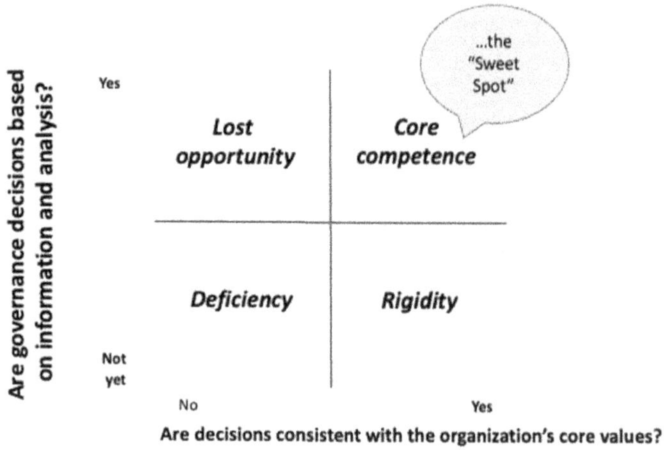

Fig. 9.1 Mapping effective governance (*Source* Created by author)

Examples in Each Quadrant

Core competence. As of late 2022, PepsiCo is one of the few established global companies that had been consistently recognized for producing superior financial returns while meeting the needs of all stakeholders. PepsiCo had always invested for the long-term and delivered results in the short-term under its Performance with Purpose (PwP) program.

Deficiency. As of late 2022, Peloton, Twitter, and WeWork were often mentioned as companies that fell off the cliff because, although they were led by highly talented and iconoclastic entrepreneurs (respectively, Jack Foley, Jack Dorsey, and Adam Neumann), these companies didn't have proper governance, that is, their boards of directors could not ask the tough questions nor figure out, how do you get the best out of a genius?

Lost opportunity. In late 2022, Meta, formerly Facebook, laid off 11,000 employees and also announced a hiring freeze as the company faced declining revenue and increased spending on a long-term multibillion dollar bet on the metaverse (virtual reality and artificial intelligence), also known as its Reality Labs hardware and software division. Meta's expenses in the third quarter of 2022 had jumped 19 percent year over year to $22.1 billion while its revenues had slipped by four percent to $27.7 billion and profits declined by 52 percent to $4.4 billion. At the time, Meta's top executive, founder and CEO Mark Zuckerberg, publicly stated that the company's metaverse investment may not pay off for a decade, but the company's board of directors remained largely silent on the matter, even though a prominent investor had written an open letter to Zuckerberg and Meta's board of directors pleading with the company to stem its Reality Labs-related losses and focus on its core, profit-generating businesses.

Rigidity. A vibrant culture of creative energy and success nurtured over decades was destroyed in the years after Time-Warner's $100 billion acquisition by AT&T in 2018. From 2019 to 2022, AT&T embarked on canceling CNN + , the $90 million "Batgirl" film, and the critically acclaimed HBO series "Westworld." For sheer strategic miscalculation and poor execution, AT&T's management of Warner Media may have no rival in recent corporate history. Yet there had been no accountability on the part of the AT&T board or shareholders. The former head of Warner Media, John Stankey, was promoted to CEO of AT&T in July 2020, and in early 2022 made uncontested decisions to spin-off DirectTV and Warner Media, even though he was in large part responsible for buying them.

To overcome deficiency, rigidity, or lost opportunity, strategists need to establish a clear sense of purpose and identity throughout their organizations. That is, members in the governance process need to instill a mindset that questions fundamental assumptions and positive perceptions of experiences, foster a psychologically safe environment where people can take interpersonal risks, and impose individual and group accountability, otherwise the organization will be static, especially during times of dynamic change or unforeseen crises (Luciano et al., 2020; Soltwisch, 2015).

Final Thoughts

Company owners, managers, and staff that came of age in the 1970s and 1980s are getting set to retire in the third and fourth decades of the twenty-first century. How a business can craft a sustainable leadership succession in a turbulent environment has become more relevant than ever before (Witt et al., 2022). Proactive planning and formalizing a governance structure for the family and business can help to ensure a smooth, successful transition to the next generation of leadership.

Successive boards of directors and executive teams will be responsible for approving and implementing the strategies for a better normal.

The upcoming generations surely need to be aware of what is worth preserving from the past and what is worth changing in the future so that an organization can stand the test of time.

End of Chapter Mini-Case: Governance at North Bay Rowing Club

Marielle MacDonell

Since its founding in Petaluma, California in 1984, the North Bay Rowing Club (NBRC) had consistently pursued its stated mission to "empower youth and adults by providing opportunities to learn and improve sweep and scull rowing skills while fostering connectivity to one another and to our unique Petaluma River environment." As a 501(c)3 non-profit organization, the NBRC envisioned "creating a community in which any individual could belong, be supported, and thrive." Rowing and competing were the club's primary activities, and the organization's core values prioritized community, socialization, and volunteerism.

After the onset of the COVID-19 pandemic in March 2020, however, NBRC was forced to shut down operations. The club's closure resulted in a severe attrition of members and coaching staff. By July 2022, club membership was at only 50 percent of the pre-pandemic level.

During summer 2022, NBRC's President Pat Hanson and her board of directors (BoD) convened a series of monthly meetings in which keeping the club afloat financially was the first order of business. Also on the agenda were longer-term organizational aspirations, such as funding for a permanent location, which would include a new boathouse and social space, as well as for scholarships that would bolster the organization's diversity program.

Operations and Marketing

Over the years, NBRC moved to four different locations on the Petaluma River. The club purchased its first facility, a shipping container named "Container #1," which was still in use at the boatyard in 2022, along

M. MacDonell
Sonoma State University, Rohnert Park, CA, USA

with four other containers that housed four- and eight-person boats, and space to add up to three additional containers for storage.

Operations of the club had also grown increasingly complex along with NBRC's increase in members, assets, and facilities. In 2022, in addition to its President and BoD, staff included a head coach, two assistant coaches, and a coach for the Learn to Row program (LTR) to teach middle-school students how to row. Searches for a primary coach for its Master-level rowing program had proven unfruitful, which meant that master rowers' practices were typically un-coached.

Other than NBRC's website, the club was present on Instagram and Facebook, used for postings about the club's Learn to Row programs and camps. On Facebook, the club had 683 followers, and 593 followers on Instagram in 2022. Outside of social media resources, many members were recruited through other members or word of mouth, yielding disappointing results in increasing membership. Outside of its social media resources, NBRC did not make any active efforts to recruit new members. In an interview in July 2022, Hanson noted, "We do not have a strong sense of self-promotion…any costs [for marketing] are minimal."

Competitive rowing typically took place during nine months over fall and spring. Like most rowing clubs, NBRC relied heavily on high school competitive members to fund its programs, but often many high school students would prioritize other sports over rowing. This caused many members to miss practices, skip seasons, or drop the sport entirely.

Competition

North Bay Rowing Club had many direct competitors in the San Francisco Bay Area and region. Fifty-two of the 91 registered clubs in California were located in Northern California, 45 within 100 miles of NBRC, and 23 within 50 miles of NBRC.[1] Many also directly competed against NBRC in rowing events. North Bay Rowing Club's most proximate competitors included Marin Rowing Association, River City Rowing Club, Capital Crew, Oakland Strokes, East Bay Rowing Club, and Lake Merritt, among which Oakland Strokes and Marin Rowing Association

[1] USRowing is a non-profit membership organization recognized by the U.S. Olympic Committee as the national governing body for the sport of rowing in the U.S.. USRowing. (n.d.). Retrieved July 26, 2022, from https://usrowing.org/sports/%202016/5/19/805_132107059777909513.

Table 9.2 Comparative club membership prices in San Francisco Bay Area, 2022

Rowing Club Programs and Membership Prices in 2022 (blank cells indicate that data were unavailable)

Program	*North Bay Rowing Club*	*Marin*	*River City*	*Capital Crew*	*Oakland Strokes*	*East Bay Rowing Club*	*Lake Merritt Rowing Club*
Masters	$500	$940–1,840	$675–775	$405		$1,740–1,920	$700
High School/ Middle School	2,645	4,800	1,320	875 –975	5,050	1,680–1,800	715
Middle School/ Learn to Row	1,375		900	1,000	3,300		
Summer Camp, per week	225	500	110	400	475		160

Source Prepared by case author from data available from competing club websites

were the largest in terms of membership. Both of these rivals consistently reported revenues of over $1.5 million versus NBRC's revenues of $141,000 in 2021 and estimated revenues of $181,000 for 2022. Indirect competitors included other water sports like kayaking, paddling, and swimming as well as land-based sports such as soccer, baseball, basketball, tennis, and pickleball. See Table 9.2, "Comparative Club Membership Prices in the San Francisco Bay Area, 2022."

NBRC's Board

North Bay Rowing Club's BoD coordinated all operations: fundraising efforts, hiring of coaches, boatyard projects, and events. As of 2022, the BoD consisted of nine volunteers; a president, vice president, secretary, treasurer, four at-large members, and a junior representative. The group met once a month to address member complaints, plan future events and projects, and coordinate the completion of tasks necessary for the various programs.

Data-Driven Decision-Making?

To kick-off the July 2022 monthly meeting, club President Hanson and her board reviewed the comparative club membership data.

The BoD proceeded to consider several options:

- **Solicit corporate sponsorships**. This would be the quickest way to get the kind of funding needed to get a community space or boathouse. If sponsored by businesses in the community, for example, it could not only create an opportunity to spread awareness of the club, but also draw in new members. This would require a large effort from the BoD or other members to attempt to attract community sponsorships.
- **Increase fundraising**. Once there is someone willing to take on the responsibilities surrounding various fundraising opportunities, increased funds would help to further improve the experience of NBRC's members. Fundraisers could be strategically marketed as a way to fund the diversity or scholarship programs the club hoped to establish.
- **Develop a recruitment strategy**. Increasing membership will increase the amount of funds the club has to work with. The addition of new members would also help work toward the level of community the club is hoping to achieve. Increased membership has the potential to lead to increased levels of diversity and scholarship programs to increase inclusivity. Greater diversity, it was felt by some board members, would also allow the club to better fund a competent coaching staff to further develop the competitive abilities of the team.
- **Adjust membership fees**. North Bay Rowing Club's revenues were very heavily linked to the success of the Junior's (high school and novice rowers) program. While fluctuations in membership occurred in all three programs during COVID, the Master and Learn to Row programs fluctuated much less, but unfortunately, the relative stability of these programs did not allow for the club to retain positive operating revenues for the 2021 fiscal year (May 2020–April 2021). While members of the Master rowing program accounted for the majority of membership, these represented only a small proportion of total club revenues.

All present at the BoD meetings were aware that, in order for NBRC to achieve short- and long-term financial stability, the organization needed to make significant progress on finding ways to increase cash flows from memberships as well as a more permanent source of capital to afford future growth. Yet there some board members remained openly opposed to the fourth option, raising membership fees, fearing that this would not only result in a loss of current members but also deter prospective members from joining the club.

Lessons learned. People who serve on boards of directors normally view their roles as being service-oriented, and they implicitly believe that board service and the interaction between directors should be positive and based on mutual respect (Boivie et al., 2021: 1680). Governance at NBRC appears to be consistent with this view, yet there were no apparent differences with respect to the composition of the executive team and the BoD (Witt et al., 2022). While trust within the boardroom, that is, among executives and directors, is critical to the functioning of any organization, absent any separation of management and governance, it is difficult to see how conflicting views about the future of NBRC could be addressed and how opposing viewpoints might eventually come into balance or consensus, especially as it relates to the strategic direction of the organization. Thus, the absence of any separation between the top management team and the BoD at the NBRC may offer critical insights into the success or failure of governance (Boivie et al., 2021: 1689).

In the words of Gersel and Johnsen (2020):

> ...managers should become familiar with a form of unstructured creative ethical deliberation very alien to the prevalent forms of cost-benefit analysis. Teaching this deliberative skill to managers will be very different from how, say, a strategy course, is currently structured. Typically, the main debate is between differing accounts of how to maximize profits. If we are right, a strategy course should also include a debate about when one should maximize profits and when the deliberative importance of profit has been diminished or disabled, such that other aims should be pursued at the expense of shareholder gains. Teaching managers to deliberate in this way will require that they are taught to consider what type of future they want to live in, what type of values their contemporary community respects, and also how various ethical ideals have historically been interpreted. (Gersel & Johnsen, 2020: 285)

To return to the 3S model presented in earlier chapters of this book, that is, the style of leadership, the situation that a company is facing, and the strategic orientation of the decision-makers is central to a debate over when it is appropriate to maximize profits and when other aims are of equal if not more importance.

End of Chapters Strategic Planning Exercises

Who is on Your Advisory Board?

Working through this book, you have had an opportunity to create your own strategic plan. Here is the final exercise.

Make a list of people that you would rely upon as a "sounding" board, for example, to provide you with advice for a career transition, deciding whether or not to follow a new opportunity, or handle a crisis. Next to each name on your list, write down each person's skills and experiences that would be of the greatest benefit in those situations.

Further Reading

Boivie, S., Withers, M. C., Graffin, S. D., & Corley, K. G. (2021). Corporate directors' implicit theories of the roles and duties of boards. *Strategic Management Journal, 42*(9), 1662–1695. https://doi.org/10.1002/smj.3320

Bonardi, J.-P., Hillman, A. J., & Keim, G. D. (2005). "The attractiveness of political markets: Implications for firm strategy. *Academy of Management Review, 30*(2), 397–413.

Clarkson, M. B. E. (1995). A stakeholder framework for analyzing and evaluating corporate social performance. *Academy of Management Review, 20*(1), 92–117.

Coulson-Thomas, C. (2021). Strategic thinking and corporate governance. *Effective Executive, 24*(4), 7–29.

Gersel, J., & Johnsen, R. (2020). Toward a novel theory of rational managerial deliberation: Stakeholders, ethical values, and corporate governance. *Academy of Management Learning & Education, 19*(3), 269–288.

Golicic, S., Signori, P., & Flint, D. F. (2015). *Contemporary wine marketing and supply chain management*. Palgrave/Macmillan.

Greiner, M., & Lee, J. (2021). US companies and political influence: How business can read the government landscape better. *Journal of Business Strategy, 42*(1), 69–75.

Hitt, M. A., Duhaime, I. M., Lyles, M. A., Aguilera, R. V., Garg, S., Hambrick, D. C., Westphal, J. D., & Wiersema, M. F. (2021). Current state and future of strategic leadership and governance theory and practice. *Academy of Management Annual Meeting Proceedings, 2021*(1), 1.

Laur, I., & Danilovic, M. (2020). Enabling change within new forms of organizations: An empirical investigation of change patterns and stakeholder influence on core intermediary activities. *Journal of Organizational Change Management, 33*(6), 1041–1070.

Le, & Lei, H. (2019). Determinants of innovation capability: The roles of transformational leadership, knowledge sharing and perceived organizational support. *Journal of Knowledge Management, 23*(3), 527–547.

Luciano, M. M., Nahrgang, J. D., & Shropshire, C. (2020). Strategic leadership systems: Viewing top management teams and boards of directors from a multiteam systems perspective. *Academy of Management Review, 45*(3), 675–701.

Morkel, A., Nienaber, H., & McNeill, R. (2021). Time for change: Tools enhancing competitive advantage in the wine business. *Journal of Global Business and Technology, 17*(2), 20–40.

Sarros, J. C., Tanewski, G. A., Winter, R. P., Santora, J. C., & Densten, I. L. (2002). Work alienation and organizational leadership. *British Journal of Management, 13*(4), 285–304.

Shane, S., & Venkataraman, S. (2000). The promise of entrepreneurship as a field of research. *Academy of Management Review, 25*(1), 217–226.

Soltwisch, B. W. (2015). The paradox of organizational rigidity. *J Leadership & Org Studies, 22*(4), 395–403.

Whelan, T., & Fink, C. (2016, October 21). The comprehensive business case for sustainability. *Harvard Business Review Digital Edition*, 2–8.

Witt, M. A., Fainshmidt, S., & Aguilera, R. V. (2022). Our board, our rules: Nonconformity to global corporate governance norms. *Administrative Science Quarterly, 67*(1), 131–166.

Index of Companies

A. Gilinsky, *Business Strategy for a Better Normal*,
https://doi.org/10.1007/978-3-031-28708-4

Index of Key Terms

A. Gilinsky, *Business Strategy for a Better Normal*,
https://doi.org/10.1007/978-3-031-28708-4

CPSIA information can be obtained
at www.ICGtesting.com
Printed in the USA
LVHW050834150523
746944LV00004BA/400

9 783031 287077